Claims *to* Fame
Fourteen Short Biographies

Book 3

Carol Einstein

Educators Publishing Service, Inc.
Cambridge and Toronto

Cover and book design by Joyce Weston

Educators Publishing Service, Inc.
31 Smith Place, Cambridge, MA 02138-1089

Printed in U.S.A.

ISBN 0-8388-2376-9

To my husband, who encouraged and
helped me every step of the way.
With thanks and love,
C.S.E.

Contents

Kent Whealy   1

Betty Robinson Schwartz   9

Robert Stevenson   18

Midori Goto   27

Gabriel García Márquez   36

Ida B. Wells   46

Janet Guthrie   56

Violet Jessop   65

George C. Wolfe   75

Rosemary Casals   84

Marie Grosholtz Tussaud   93

William Karesh   102

Fannie Spelce   112

John Harrison   122

Acknowledgments

To those no longer here: Bernice Einstein,
Recha Einstein-Weil, and Julie Weil.

To my colleagues, friends, and family: Joan Amron, Bonnie Tibuzi Caputo, Susanna Einstein, Maureen Farbstein, Bonnie Long, Jill Mehler, and Charles Thompson. You were always willing to listen and to help. With special thanks to my skillful and understanding editor, Mary Troeger, who always catches my errors and clarifies my thoughts.

New York City

Dear Reader,

Before you start reading these stories, I want to tell you how I came to write this book. When I was your age, I always loved hearing family stories about the interesting things my grandmother and great aunts did when they were young. I also loved reading stories about real people who had lived before I was born. When I grew up and started working with children, many of my students said they wished there were more books telling about women who had lived long ago. Then my students told me they would like some of the stories to be about men, too, and about people living right now. So in this book you will find all of these kinds of stories.

I hope that you enjoy reading them and find these lives as interesting as I did.

Carol Einstein

What do you need to do to make a good garden?

_____

_____

Courtesy of Kent Whealy

Kent Whealy
1946–

When Kent Whealy was growing up in Wellington, Kansas, he often helped his parents take care of their vegetable garden. But he never dreamed that one day he would devote his life to working with gardens and different kinds of rare seeds.

How did Whealy, who had studied **journalism** at the University of Kansas, ever get involved with looking after seeds? At first, after graduating from college, he worked in a number of different jobs. Then in 1971, the grandfather of his wife, Diane, became ill with **leukemia.** Grandpa Ott wanted to spend the rest of his days on his farm in Decorah, Iowa, but he could not do this without someone helping him. The Whealys moved to the Decorah farm so that they could care for him. Grandpa Ott lived just one more year, but during that time he showed Kent and Diane many of the things he knew about gardening.

"He taught us a lot," says Whealy. "He also gave us seeds of two plants that his parents had brought from Bavaria in the 1870s. One was a large, pink German tomato; the other was a beautiful, little purple morning glory with a red star in its throat." Grandpa Ott asked them to take good care of these **heirloom** seeds.

When Grandpa Ott died in the winter, the Whealys realized that if the seeds were to survive for future generations, they would have to take care of them. Kent remembers that just around that time he and Diane had read several articles by well-known scientists who wrote of their concern that the seeds for basic food crops might die out. Losing such seeds forever would cause terrible problems all over the world. Whealy explains, "Any variety is **susceptible** to attack, at some point in the future, from a disease or pest that we may not even know about yet." He and Diane understood that if they could preserve the old plant varieties, these could be grown and used by others.

The Whealys began looking for people who were also keeping heirloom seeds. They discovered that many elderly gardeners and farmers were growing a wide range of plants from almost unknown varieties of seeds. These plants produced plenty of vegetables, fruits, and grains and had a delicious flavor. Kent and Diane learned that in the past many people who had come to the United States and Canada as **immigrants** had brought their best seeds with them. They often hid them in the linings of their suitcases, under the bands of their hats, or even sewed them into the hems of their dresses. Whealy realized that those seeds from earlier generations existed in much greater numbers than what was offered through seed catalogs. He also realized that these heirloom seeds had never been collected in an organized way.

So in 1975, the Whealys started the Seed Savers Exchange, a not-for-profit organization. At first, there were twenty-nine members, who offered a few dozen types of seeds through a newsletter. Today, the Seed Savers Exchange offers 11,000 rare varieties through the 450-page Seed Savers Yearbook, which is sent to 8,000 gardeners. Over the years the members of the Seed Savers Exchange have distributed about 750,000 samples of rare seeds that were often close to extinction and were not usually found in commercial catalogues.

In 1986, Kent and Diane started Heritage Farm in Iowa, which takes care of and displays a collection of 18,000 heirloom vegetables. Each summer the seeds of almost 2,000 varieties are multiplied in Heritage Farm's large organic Preservation Gardens. Whealy's aim is to get these heirloom plants out into gardens all across North America. This is the only way to make sure the plants survive.

Kent Whealy is delighted that through the Seed Savers Exchange he can help a gardener get seeds that are part of American history. There are seeds that were first grown by Native North Americans, seeds brought over on the Mayflower, and seeds that Thomas Jefferson grew in his gardens. Kent says, "There has never been a more exciting time to be a gardener!"

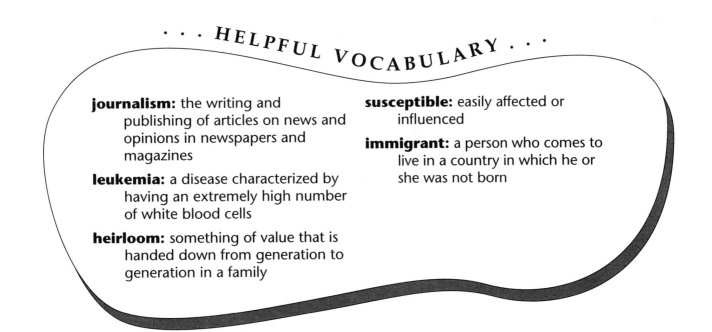

· · · HELPFUL VOCABULARY · · ·

journalism: the writing and publishing of articles on news and opinions in newspapers and magazines

leukemia: a disease characterized by having an extremely high number of white blood cells

heirloom: something of value that is handed down from generation to generation in a family

susceptible: easily affected or influenced

immigrant: a person who comes to live in a country in which he or she was not born

THINKING ABOUT WHAT YOU HAVE READ

1. Where was Kent Whealy raised?

_____

2. Why did Whealy move to Grandpa Ott's farm?

_____

_____

_____

3. What did Grandpa Ott ask Diane and Kent to do?

_____

_____

_____

4. What did Whealy discover when he began searching for other people who owned heirloom seeds?

_____

_____

5. What made him decide to devote his life to taking care of seeds?

_____

_____

_____

6. What is the goal of the Seed Savers Exchange?

_____

_____

7. Today, how does the Seed Savers Exchange help gardeners?

_____

_____

8. How could you help heirloom plants survive?

_____

_____

_____

WORKING WITH WORDS

What three new words did you learn from this story?

_____   _____   _____

Try to use two of them in sentences.

_____

_____

_____

A **proverb** is a short saying that expresses something that many people believe to be true. "Every cloud has a silver lining" is a proverb. It means that sometimes something good can come from something bad.

Explain how Grandpa Ott's illness is an example of this proverb.

_____

_____

_____

Kent Whealy thinks that the proverb "Waste not, want not" is true. What do you think this proverb means?

_____

_____

_____

An **antonym** is a word that has the opposite meaning of another word. _High_ is the antonym of _low_. Write an antonym for each of these words. Give yourself a bonus point if you can do more than six.

often   _____   graceful   _____

spend   _____   sweet   _____

future   _____   rare   _____

elderly   _____   destroy   _____

WRITING SKILLS

Imagine that Kent Whealy is going to speak at your school. Write a paragraph about him for your school newspaper. Be sure that your paragraph has a topic sentence, which gives the main idea of the paragraph, and a concluding sentence, which lets the reader know that you have finished your discussion.

First, write down some key ideas you want to talk about. When you have finished your paragraph, proofread your writing. Check it for correct spelling, grammar, capitalization, and punctuation.

Key ideas:

_____

_____

_____

Kent Whealy Speaks at _____

_____

_____

_____

_____

_____

_____

_____

Imagine that you are an immigrant traveling to the United States. You are worried that you will not be allowed to keep some seeds you are bringing from your native land, so you hide them. Describe your trip to the United States. Are you excited? Are you scared? Who is traveling with you?

Before you begin, write down some key ideas. When you have finished your story, proofread your writing. Check it for correct spelling, grammar, capitalization, and punctuation.

Key ideas:

_____

_____

_____

Story

_____

_____

_____

_____

_____

_____

_____

_____

_____

Bettman/Corbis

Betty Robinson Schwartz
1911–1999

Sometimes something happens just by chance, and it changes your life forever. That is just what happened to Betty Robinson, track's first female Olympic gold medalist. Robinson was born in Riverdale, Illinois, a small town south of Chicago. When she was sixteen years old, Robinson was running to catch a departing commuter train. Charles Price, a high school teacher and assistant track coach in Harvey, Illinois, saw her dashing for the train. He could not believe how quickly she was running. (According to **legend,** she caught the train.) Price went looking for Robinson, and when he found her, he said, "You can run, Betty." He asked her to run fifty yards for him in a school corridor, and with that trial her track career began.

In the late 1920s, women's track-and-field events were just beginning in the United States. Years later Robinson told a reporter, "I had no idea that women even ran then. I grew up a **hick**. That is when I found out that they actually had track meets for women."

Three weeks after Robinson had been spotted running for a train, she made her racing **debut** at a regional meet and finished second to Helen Rilkey, the woman who held the United States record for fastest time at 100 meters. In her next meet, the Chicago-area Olympic trials, Robinson equaled the world record of 100 meters at 12.0 seconds. (Today's world record is 10.49 seconds, which was set in 1988.) Robinson traveled to Newark, New Jersey, for her third meet, the United States final Olympic trials. She finished second and made the Olympic team.

The first year that women track-and-field athletes were allowed to compete in the Olympics was 1928. Robinson and her teammates sailed to Amsterdam, in the Netherlands, where the Olympics were being held. To stay in good condition during the ship's voyage, she and the other members of the Olympic team used a **linoleum** track, which was laid out on the ship's deck for their workouts.

Just four months after she took up the sport, Robinson was running in the Olympics; this would be only the fourth meet of her career. She finished second in her trial meet and first in her semifinal meet. Robinson was the only American to reach the finals. The last race was very close, but Robinson, with a time of 12.2 seconds, was declared the winner over a favored Canadian runner, Fanny Rosenfeld. Because the 100-meter race was the first of five women's track-and-field events at the 1928 Olympic Games, Robinson's gold medal was the first one ever awarded in her sport. Later she said, "When the flag went up after the race, I started crying like a baby."

Robinson returned from the Olympics to ticker-tape parades in New York and Chicago. She received a diamond watch from her hometown fans and a silver cup from her high school.

In 1931, while Robinson was still an outstanding athlete, she was in a terrible plane crash. Her eighteen-year-old cousin had been piloting the small plane. Both women survived, but Robinson was badly injured. She was unconscious for seven weeks and was in the hospital for eleven weeks. Her leg was in a hip-to-heel cast; for four months, she was in a wheelchair or on crutches. The leg became a half-inch shorter. Robinson said, "If I had not been in such good physical condition, I would not have lived through it." In time, she returned to college and began once more to work on her running.

It was three and a half years before she was able to compete again. In 1936, Robinson tried a comeback. Because of her injuries she could not bend a knee, so she had to make a standing rather than a crouching start in the 100-meter race. In spite of this disadvantage, she was able to make the Olympic relay team and was chosen to run the third leg, or section, of the race. At the Olympic Games the American team won first place when a member of the record-setting German team **fumbled** the baton pass before the last handoff. Robinson had made an unbelievable comeback.

In 1939, she married Richard S. Schwartz. After Robinson stopped running, she remained active in track as a coach, a timer, and a fund-raiser for a new group of Olympic athletes. Besides working at a local hardware store, she concentrated on raising her two children. Many years after she stopped running, Robinson said, "It happened so long ago. I still can't believe the attention I get for something I did so long ago."

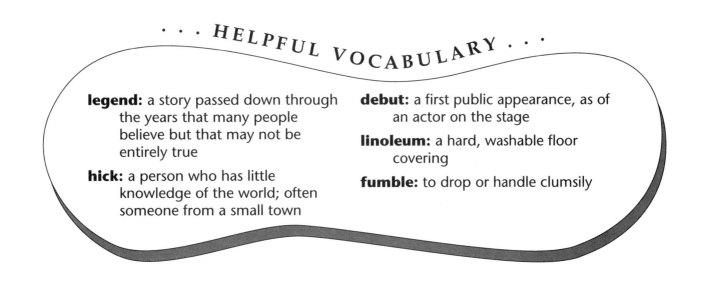

· · · HELPFUL VOCABULARY · · ·

legend: a story passed down through the years that many people believe but that may not be entirely true

hick: a person who has little knowledge of the world; often someone from a small town

debut: a first public appearance, as of an actor on the stage

linoleum: a hard, washable floor covering

fumble: to drop or handle clumsily

THINKING ABOUT WHAT YOU HAVE READ

1. Who was track's first female Olympic gold medalist?

_____

_____

2. What happened to Betty Robinson when she was sixteen years old?

_____

_____

_____

3. When did women start competing in track-and-field events in the Olympics?

_____

_____

_____

4. Since Betty Robinson began competing, how has the training for major sports events changed?

_____

_____

_____

5. How do we know that Betty Robinson was a natural athlete?

_____

_____

_____

6. Why do you think Robinson began crying when the American flag was raised at the Olympics?

_____

_____

7. How did Robinson's excellent physical shape help her recover after the plane crash?

_____

_____

WORKING WITH WORDS

Sometimes words have more than one meaning. In the following sentences, the word in bold print has one meaning. Write what it is. Then write another meaning the word may have.

Example: You have **neat** handwriting. In the sentence, *neat* means "orderly or tidy." *Neat* can also mean "done in a clever way."

Sometimes something happens just by **chance.**

_____

_____

_____

Robinson had been **spotted** running for the train.

_____

_____

_____

In the fourth **meet** of her career, she ran in the Olympics.

_____

_____

_____

She finished second in her **trial** meet.

_____

_____

_____

A **synonym** is a word that has the same or almost the same meaning as another word. *Rich* and *wealthy* are synonyms. Think of synonyms for the words that follow. See if you can write two.

outstanding   _____   _____

beginning   _____   _____

voyage   _____   _____

quickly   _____   _____

natural   _____   _____

next   _____   _____

A **simile** is a phrase or expression introduced by the words *like* or *as;* it compares two things that are not alike. Robinson used a simile when she said, "I started crying *like a baby.*" Explain what this simile means. Then see if you can use the simile in a sentence.

_____

_____

_____

Now explain what these similes mean and use them in sentences. Give yourself a bonus point if you can do the last one.

Robinson streaked *like lightning* to the finish line.

_____

_____

_____

Betty was *pleased as Punch* when she won her second Olympic medal.

_____

_____

_____

WRITING SKILLS

Betty's running talents were discovered by chance. Write about a time when you or someone you know found out something by chance.

_____

_____

_____

_____

_____

_____

_____

_____

Betty was a determined person. She would not give up. Write a paragraph about "Determined Betty." Be sure that your paragraph has a topic sentence, which gives the main idea of the paragraph, and a concluding sentence, which lets the reader know that you have finished your discussion.

First, write down some key ideas. When you have finished your paragraph, proofread your writing. Check it for correct spelling, grammar, capitalization, and punctuation.

Key ideas:

_____

_____

_____

Determined Betty

_____

_____

_____

_____

_____

_____

_____

_____

_____

Courtesy of The National Galleries of Scotland, Edinburgh

Robert Stevenson
1772–1850

Many people have heard of Robert Louis Stevenson, the author of *Treasure Island*. But too few people know about his grandfather, Robert Stevenson, who faced terrible weather and rocky coastlines to design and build lighthouses around Scotland. These lighthouses saved the lives of thousands of sailors whose ships would have been broken on the rocks and hidden **reefs** that are scattered along the Scottish coast.

Stevenson was born in Glasgow, Scotland. When he was two years old, his father died, leaving his mother with very little money. Because she wanted her son to have a good education, Mrs. Stevenson moved to Edinburgh when he was six years old.

By the time Stevenson was a teenager, his mother had married Thomas Smith. Smith owned an **ironworks,** where he made lamps and designed street lighting for Edinburgh. At that time, lamps used oil, which gave out only a weak light. But Smith thought of placing a thin piece of mirror behind the light as a reflector. His design made the lights four times stronger. Stevenson loved to visit the ironworks and, by the age of eighteen, was happily working there, making lamplights and grates. He also studied engineering at Glasgow University.

In the 1700s, sailors did not have the equipment we have today for **navigation.** The seas around Scotland were very dangerous. In order for a sailor to bring a ship safely to shore he had to be able to recognize the coastline. At night, of course, this was not possible. The only help for ships near Scotland during a storm or in darkness was one coal-fire light on the east coast, and it was often put out by rain. Because many people were upset about the dangers of the Scottish coast, the government set up the Northern Lighthouse Board to find a way to reduce the number of shipwrecks.

Thomas Smith was looking for other uses for his lights with reflectors and suggested that the Lighthouse Board try them. He explained that the lamps would be protected by glass and that the lamplight would be purer and brighter than light produced from coal. Joined with the reflectors, the lights could be seen at a great distance. From on board ship, it would be impossible to mistake them for any other light on shore. The Board was convinced. They appointed Smith to be their engineer and told him to build four lighthouses.

Stevenson was very excited about his stepfather's new job, and during his school vacations he helped Smith put in the four lights. Within a few years, they were partners. When Thomas Smith retired, the Northern Lighthouse Board appointed Stevenson to replace his stepfather as engineer.

Stevenson would build twenty-three more lighthouses along the coast of Scotland. Since the forces of the wind, the waves, and the tide on a lighthouse were so great, Stevenson decided to build each lighthouse of rock, with walls at least nine feet thick at the base. At first, he used oil lamps with reflectors, but later he also used gas lamps.

Building and keeping up the lighthouses was not easy. Those that were constructed on rocks several miles from land needed special planning to bring the workmen and the materials to the spot where the lighthouse would be built. Stevenson had to make long, dangerous sea voyages to supervise each step of their construction. Even the lighthouses that were on the mainland were difficult to build. The materials had to be carried by horseback over miles of empty, uneven land to the building spot. Only one trip a day was possible because of the rough conditions. When the lighthouses were finished, Stevenson had to teach people how to put in and work the lights and then how to take care of them.

Over the years, many people were against building the lighthouses. Some people said that they would not be **visible** when needed, and some thought they were too expensive. But the worst threat came from the wreckers, people who wanted the ships to be destroyed. Many people living in coastal villages made a living by using or selling the materials and goods that washed up on shore from wrecked ships.

In spite of these problems, Stevenson knew how important it was to build and take care of the lighthouses. He enjoyed living the life of a lighthouse **pioneer**, with its hard work and adventure. He also loved the sea voyage he made each year around the coast to inspect all of the lighthouses.

In 1842, when he was seventy years old, he retired. While he could no longer carry out all the duties of chief engineer, he still made his yearly visit to see the lighthouses. By that time, too, three of his sons were continuing his work.

Then, in 1850, as Stevenson was preparing for his yearly inspection trip, his sons told him that they felt he was just not well enough to go. Soon afterwards he died. Today many things about ships and navigation have changed, but Stevenson's lighthouses still stand as a living monument to their builder.

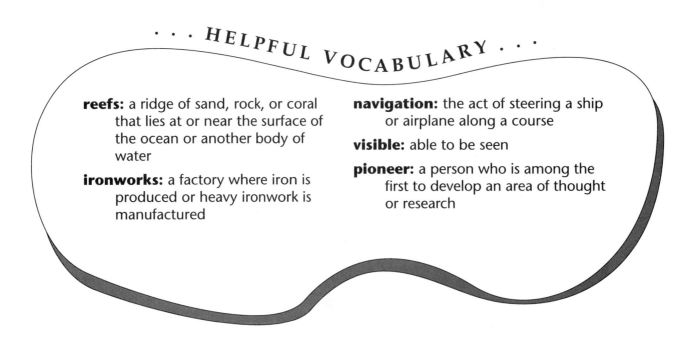

· · · HELPFUL VOCABULARY · · ·

reefs: a ridge of sand, rock, or coral that lies at or near the surface of the ocean or another body of water

ironworks: a factory where iron is produced or heavy ironwork is manufactured

navigation: the act of steering a ship or airplane along a course

visible: able to be seen

pioneer: a person who is among the first to develop an area of thought or research

THINKING ABOUT WHAT YOU HAVE READ

1. Who was Robert Louis Stevenson?

_____

_____

2. When Robert Stevenson was a teenager, what did he do?

_____

_____

3. In the late 1700s, why was traveling by sea near Scotland so unsafe?

_____

_____

_____

4. How did Thomas Smith improve the lighting in the city of Edinburgh?

_____

_____

_____

5. For sailors, what was the greatest advantage of Smith's lighting system?

_____

_____

_____

6. How many lighthouses did Stevenson build around Scotland?

_____

_____

7. Why was Stevenson's job dangerous?

_____

_____

8. Why were some people against building the lighthouses?

_____

_____

_____

WORKING WITH WORDS

How many describing words can you think of that tell what Robert Stevenson's job was like? Try to think of at least three.

_____   _____   _____

_____   _____   _____

Look at the phrases below. On the lines write a sentence using each of the words in bold print. Give yourself a bonus point if you can do more than three.

Example: lighthouse **pioneer**. A pioneer must be a very brave person.

rocky coastlines

_____

_____

put out by rain

_____

_____

yearly voyage

_____

_____

hidden **reefs**

_____

_____

living **monument**

_____

_____

Some words sound alike but are spelled differently and have different meanings. These words are called **homophones.**

Example: *plain* and *plane.* I like *plain* cake. Was your *plane* on time?

See if you can fill in the blanks with homophones. Be sure to read all the sentences in each group before you write your answers.

Even though there were shipwrecks, people _____ travel by sea.

The house burned down quickly because it was made of _____.

Stevenson had _____ wait _____ long for his supplies to come.

_____ plus four is six.

The _____ purpose of building lighthouses was to save lives.

_____ is a New England state.

The horse has a thick _____.

_____ people thought that building lighthouses was important.

What is the _____ of twenty-eight and ninety-two?

Stevenson's sons said he was too _____ to go on the trip.

What _____ does your vacation start?

Stevenson stood on the beach and watched the _____ go out.

The young child slowly _____ his shoelaces.

WRITING SKILLS

Robert Stevenson's work made the world safer in the 1800s. What do you think could be invented that would make the world safer now? Explain why your invention is needed and how it would help.

_____

_____

_____

_____

_____

_____

_____

An **expanded paragraph** is a full-length paragraph that lets you give as much information as you like about each one of your supporting ideas. So that your meaning is clear, you should separate your supporting ideas with transitions. A **transition word** gives the reader the signal that you have finished discussing one idea and are ready to move to the next idea. These are common transition words.

first   second   next   last   finally

Imagine you are a news reporter writing about the dangers of traveling by sea to Scotland. Write an expanded paragraph about these dangers. Try to use at least three of the transition words above. Be sure that your paragraph has a topic sentence, which gives the main idea of the paragraph, and a concluding sentence, which lets the reader know that you have finished your discussion.

First, write down some key ideas. When you have finished your paragraph, proofread your writing. Check it for correct spelling, grammar, capitalization, and punctuation.

Key ideas:

_____

_____

_____

_____

The Dangers of Traveling by Sea to Scotland

_____

_____

_____

_____

_____

_____

_____

_____

_____

_____

What are some things you do to help other people?

_____

_____

Photo by Susan Johann

Midori Goto
1971–

Why does Midori Goto, the world-famous violinist, take time to play music in many schools each year? She says she wants to help children learn to love music. "I love children, I love music, and I wanted to find a way to connect the two." So when she was twenty years old, she set up Midori & Friends, a **foundation** whose goal is to bring music into children's lives.

Midori was born in Osaka, Japan. Her father was an engineer, and her mother was a violinist. At age two, Midori asked for a violin, which she received on her third birthday. When she was four years old, her mother started teaching her how to play. Because Mrs. Goto was working, Midori often had to practice by herself. She remembers that when her mother came home, "she was cooking and I would practice in the kitchen." Then in 1979, an American friend of Mrs. Goto's made a tape of Midori playing. A famous music teacher at the Juilliard School of Music in New York City, Dorothy DeLay, heard the tape and offered Midori a scholarship to the Aspen Music Festival in Colorado, where she made her debut. Many famous musicians who were at Aspen that summer **raved** about her musical ability. She was so talented at such a young age that they began to call her a **prodigy.**

In 1982, Mrs. Goto decided to move to New York City so that Midori could study music with Dorothy DeLay at Juilliard. Besides getting used to a new country, Midori had to handle both her schoolwork and her musical studies. She was very busy. At first, she performed only eight or ten times a year, playing pieces that were carefully chosen to help her develop her musical skills.

Then, on a hot, humid day in July 1986, fourteen-year-old Midori suddenly became famous. She was playing the **solo** violin part in Leonard Bernstein's *Serenade,* at the Tanglewood Music Festival, in Massachusetts. Bernstein was conducting the orchestra. While Midori was playing, the string broke on her violin. Thinking quickly, she switched instruments with a violinist in the orchestra. But a string on *that* violin broke, too, so she switched instruments again with another player in the orchestra. Even with all the confusion, Midori did not miss a note. At the end of the performance, the audience went wild and Bernstein hugged Midori. The next day she was on the front page of the *New York Times.*

Today, Midori is a professional musician with a demanding touring schedule that takes her all over the world. Even though she is very busy, she also works hard for Midori & Friends. When she first started the foundation, Midori did everything herself. "I went to the office, typed all the letters, worked on the computer." But since then the organization has grown and now has a full-time staff.

Through her foundation, Midori brings professional musicians into the public elementary and junior high schools to **inspire** and teach children. The musicians play different kinds of music (classical and jazz) and different kinds of instruments (wind, brass, and strings). They usually give both demonstrations and concerts.

In addition, the foundation offers children a program of music lessons on different instruments. Midori is excited about children learning to play music. "We send in teachers and we give children group lessons. We rent instruments and lend them out to them, all free of charge." In the spring, the children themselves give a concert in their school.

When she is not touring, Midori enjoys the concerts she gives at the schools. Afterwards, the children ask her questions. Like Midori, some of the students were born outside the United States. "I'm sure it makes a difference to the kids that I'm an Asian-American. Often I get asked about things they are struggling with, like when did I come here, and how did I learn English."

Midori says, "These children accept me as a friend, accept my music. That's what draws me to do this." Midori, through her foundation, has brought music instruction back to some public schools that could no longer afford to offer it. One principal says, "What she has done you couldn't begin to pay for."

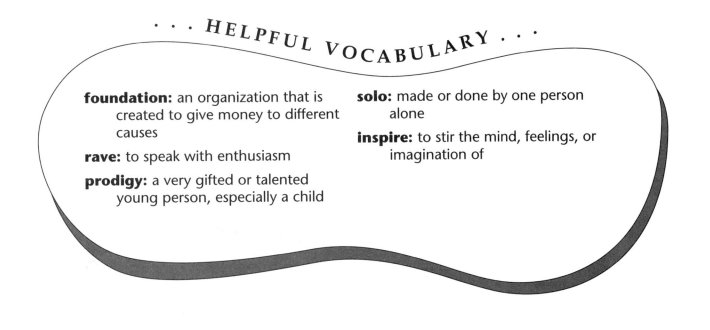

· · · HELPFUL VOCABULARY · · ·

foundation: an organization that is created to give money to different causes

rave: to speak with enthusiasm

prodigy: a very gifted or talented young person, especially a child

solo: made or done by one person alone

inspire: to stir the mind, feelings, or imagination of

THINKING ABOUT WHAT YOU HAVE READ

1. Who first taught Midori to play the violin?

_____

_____

2. Why was Midori given a violin?

_____

_____

3. What do you think it feels like to be a prodigy?

_____

_____

4. How did Midori end up at the Aspen Music Festival?

_____

_____

_____

5. Why was July 1986 an important month for Midori?

_____

_____

_____

6. How does Midori help children?

_____

_____

7. What do you think Midori was like as a child?

_____

_____

8. If Midori & Friends offered music lessons at your school, what
   instrument would you like to learn to play?

_____

_____

_____

WORKING WITH WORDS

What three new words did you learn from this story?

_____   _____   _____

Try to use two of them in sentences.

_____

_____

_____

A **suffix** is a letter or group of letters that we place at the end of a word or word root to change its meaning. The suffix -_ful_ means "full of."

Example: _helpful_. Midori wanted to _help_ children. She was very _helpful_.

List three words and then make new words by adding the suffix -_ful_.

play   **playful**

_____   _____

_____   _____

_____   _____

The suffix -_less_ means "without." List three words and then make new words by adding the suffix -_less_.

use   **useless**

_____   _____

_____   _____

_____   _____

Look at the words *bracelet* and *necklace.* They belong to the same general class or group. Both are pieces of jewelry. They differ from each other in that one is worn on the wrist and the other is worn on the neck. Now look at the following pairs of words. Write down what class or group they belong to. Then write one way in which they are different. Give yourself a bonus point if you can do the last one.

violin—drum

_____

_____

_____

musician—conductor

_____

_____

_____

orchestra—choir

_____

_____

_____

drawing—painting

_____

_____

_____

WRITING SKILLS

Think about the concert at Tanglewood in 1986. Pretend you are Midori or Leonard Bernstein. Write a letter to a friend, telling what happened during the concert. In your letter describe what you did and what you thought; use details from the story.

First, write down some key ideas. When you have finished your paragraph, proofread your writing. Check it for correct spelling, grammar, capitalization, and punctuation.

Key ideas:

_____

_____

_____

Dear _____,

_____

_____

_____

_____

_____

_____

Sincerely,

_____

When Midori was a child, she moved from Japan to the United States. How do you think she felt when she learned she was moving? What things would she miss in Japan? What things would she look forward to in the United States?

First, write down some key ideas. When you have finished your paragraph, proofread your writing. Check your writing for correct spelling, grammar, capitalization, and punctuation.

Key ideas:

_____

_____

_____

Paragraph

_____

_____

_____

_____

_____

_____

_____

_____

_____

Bettman/Corbis

Gabriel García Márquez
1928–

Gabriel García Márquez, or "Gabo" as he is called by many in the Spanish-speaking world, is a national hero in Colombia. Who is he and what has he done to earn such respect? García Márquez is a writer, and he often speaks out for human rights.

García Márquez was born in Aracataca, a run-down town on the north coast of Colombia, where his mother's family lived. Because of a quarrel between his grandfather and his father, his parents moved to a town two hundred miles away, shortly after his birth. They left their son in Aracataca where he was raised by his grandparents and three aunts, who lived together in a large, **gloomy** house. The area was rich in history and legend, and García Márquez's family members were born storytellers. His grandfather, a retired colonel, would tell him stories about battles he had fought in and about the old days when Aracataca was a wealthy town. His grandmother and aunts would often tell him tales about ghosts, spirits, and dead **ancestors.** García Márquez loved listening to their stories.

When he was nine years old, he went to live with his parents in Sucre. At school, he often drew comics; he thinks he did this because he wanted to tell stories but was too young to write them down. Later his parents sent him to a public boarding school for gifted students in Zipaquirá, a small town near Bogotá. At school, he felt that he did not fit in; often he was lonely. But he did discover that he was good at writing and that he enjoyed it.

Wanting to please his parents, García Márquez began taking classes in law at the University of Bogotá. But instead of studying, he started to write. He was delighted when a national newspaper, *El Espectador,* published his first short stories and praised him as a new and talented writer. After quitting law studies, he worked as a journalist in Barranquilla and later in Bogotá. During the day he wrote a daily newspaper column, and at night he worked on his short stories.

In 1955, García Márquez wrote several articles that exposed lies of the Colombian government. Because his boss was afraid the government might punish García Márquez, he sent him on assignment to Europe. After working and traveling in Europe for two years, García Márquez returned to Colombia for a short time to marry Mercedes Barcha. During the next few years, García Márquez, with his wife and newborn child, lived in several different countries, where he worked as a journalist. Then in 1961, they settled in Mexico City.

One day in 1965, as García Márquez was driving with his family, the complete first chapter of a novel about a **dictator** suddenly came to him. He brought his family home immediately and put Mercedes in charge of everything. For the next eighteen months, he wrote for eight to ten hours a day to finish his novel *One Hundred Years of Solitude.*

In this book, García Márquez blended history and imagination. Setting the story in the imaginary community of Macondo, he traced the lives of several generations of one family. Besides including folk tales and ghost stories like the ones he had listened to as a child, he also expressed many of the problems of South America.

When the book was finished, García Márquez did not have enough money to mail it to his publisher, who was in Argentina. To pay the postage, Mercedes sold her hair dryer and their electric heater. Even then they could not afford to mail the whole manuscript all at once, so it was sent in two separate packages.

The response to the book was amazing. The publisher printed eight thousand copies, which were sold out in a week, mostly at newsstands in subway stations in Buenos Aires, Argentina. Once the book was translated into other languages, readers around the world rushed to buy it. Both readers and critics called it a masterpiece. The book has now been translated into more than thirty languages and has sold about thirty million copies. García Márquez suddenly became the most famous living Latin American writer.

In the years that followed, he continued to write novels, short stories, and newspaper articles. In 1982, he was awarded the Nobel Prize for Literature. With the money he has received from his books and prizes, he has supported causes he believes in. To many Colombians, Gabriel García Márquez is a symbol of national pride, and his opinions are respected throughout Latin America. His **prestige** is so great that both governments and **rebels** trust him. He has worked to end the civil wars in El Salvador and Nicaragua and has helped gain the release of hostages kidnapped by various groups in Colombia.

García Márquez continues to live most of the year in Mexico City. The rest of the time he and his wife stay in their homes in other countries. Each place is furnished in the same way—white carpets, large glass coffee tables, modern art, a carefully chosen sound system, and an identical computer. García Márquez says that this makes it possible for him to work wherever he is.

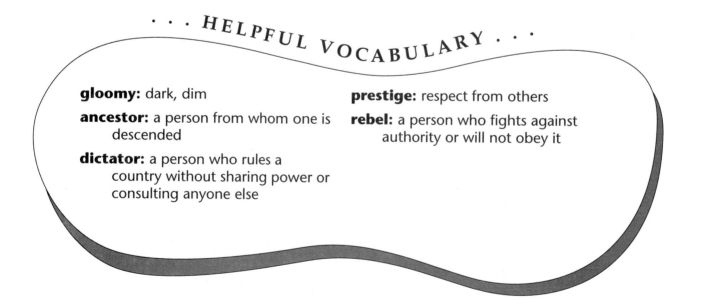

· · · HELPFUL VOCABULARY · · ·

gloomy: dark, dim

ancestor: a person from whom one is descended

dictator: a person who rules a country without sharing power or consulting anyone else

prestige: respect from others

rebel: a person who fights against authority or will not obey it

THINKING ABOUT WHAT YOU HAVE READ

1. Why do many people respect Gabriel García Márquez?

_____

_____

2. How did his experiences as a child help him later as a writer?

_____

_____

_____

3. When he was a child, why did García Márquez love drawing comics ?

_____

_____

_____

4. What is Aracataca?

_____

_____

_____

5. What was so special about a car ride that García Márquez took in 1965?

_____

_____

_____

6. Why was it not easy for him to send *One Hundred Years of Solitude* to his publisher?

_____

_____

_____

7. When someone becomes famous quickly, we say the person became famous "overnight." How did García Márquez become famous "overnight"?

_____

_____

_____

8. How has García Márquez helped other people?

_____

_____

_____

WORKING WITH WORDS

How many describing words can you think of that tell what García Márquez was like as a child? Try to think of at least three.

_____   _____   _____

_____   _____   _____

A **definition** explains the meaning of a word or group of words. A definition of the word _generous_ is willing and happy to share.

Try to write a good definition for the following words:

hero

_____

run-down

_____

awarded

_____

blended

_____

talented

_____

How are an ostrich, a crow, a hawk, an owl, and a parrot alike? If you said they are all birds, you are correct. Now read the following sets of words and explain how they are alike.

Superman   The Simpsons   Betty and Veronica
Looney Tunes   Spiderman

_____

_____

Cinderella   Snow White   Hansel and Gretel   Peter Pan
Little Red Riding Hood

_____

_____

Newsweek   Sports Illustrated   Time   Life   Nickelodeon

_____

_____

American flag   skunk   tiger   candy cane   zebra

_____

_____

Now list your own set of words and explain how the words are alike.

_____

_____

_____

_____

WRITING SKILLS

Gabriel García Márquez often uses his relatives as models for characters in his stories. Does someone in your family have a terrific sense of humor? Is someone always playing jokes? Is there a person who is very kind or brave? Describe a member of your family who you think would make a good character in a story.

_____

_____

_____

_____

_____

_____

_____

Gabriel García Márquez tells stories in which magical things happen to people in their everyday life. Think of a story you would like to tell that has some magic in it and write it down. Be sure that your story has a beginning, a middle, and an ending. Remember that including specific details makes your story more interesting.

First, write down some key ideas. When you have finished your story, proofread your writing. Check it for correct spelling, grammar, capitalization, and punctuation. Then make a picture to illustrate your story.

Key ideas:

_____

_____

_____

Story

Picture

What does it mean when we say a person is brave?

_____

_____

Courtesy of The University of Chicago

Ida B. Wells
1862—1931

It took great courage to speak out against **lynching**. One of the first
and strongest opponents of lynch mobs was a woman, Ida B. Wells.

When Wells was born in July 1862, in Holly Springs, Mississippi, her
parents were slaves. Just six months later President Abraham Lincoln
signed the Emancipation Proclamation, which freed all slaves. Wells's
parents taught her that African Americans had the right to live and work
where they wanted.

She was just fourteen when her parents died in a yellow-fever
epidemic. To support herself and her five brothers and sisters, Wells took
a job teaching school for twenty-five dollars a week.

Later, she moved to Memphis, Tennessee, where she taught in one of the city's African-American schools. In this growing Southern city, Wells saw how unfairly African Americans were treated, and she experienced discrimination herself.

She decided to fight to change things in Memphis. While she continued teaching, she began writing articles about race and politics in the South for the African-American newspapers in Memphis. She also bought a part interest in one African-American newspaper, the *Free Speech.*

Her articles, which she signed with the name Iola, were so good that they were regularly reprinted in African-American newspapers in other parts of the country. By 1892, she was earning enough money to buy a larger share in the paper.

Then three African-American men, who were Wells's friends, were lynched in Memphis, but no one was arrested and no one was punished. So Wells began investigating and **publicizing** facts about lynching. This was a subject people were afraid to discuss. She knew that her friends had been lynched because their grocery store was taking business from a grocery store owned by a white man. Wells realized that lynching served a clear purpose. It gave people an excuse to frighten African Americans, especially those who were gaining wealth and property.

For the next two months, Wells traveled throughout the South to collect as many facts as she could about other lynchings. She asked both whites and African Americans to tell her the details in each case. This was very dangerous work because the people who had carried out the lynchings did not want anyone asking questions. More than once, Wells thought she would be attacked by the people she talked with.

When she returned to Memphis, Wells wrote a story for the front page of the *Free Speech;* she gave many facts about other lynchings. Then she left for a meeting in New York. As soon as she arrived in the North, she learned that a mob of angry white men had smashed the printing press and ruined the furniture at the newspaper office. The men left a warning for the owners of the paper—if they started publishing again, they would be killed. When the white men discovered that Wells was the author of the article, they said she would be killed on sight.

Wells decided not to return to the South. She stayed in New York and began writing news articles for the *New York Age.* One of her first articles was a large front-page story giving the dates, the locations, and the names of the victims of several dozen lynchings. Then Wells traveled to many major cities in the North, making speeches about the evil of lynching and organizing groups to fight it.

In 1895, Wells married Ferdinand Barnett, a Chicago lawyer and newspaper editor. In the same year, she published *A Red Record*. This was the first detailed report on lynching ever to be printed. After her marriage, Wells gave up some of her traveling so that she could spend time raising her six children. But she worked until the end of her life to improve the lives of African Americans. In a time when very few people spoke out against lynching, Ida B. Wells had the courage to take a stand.

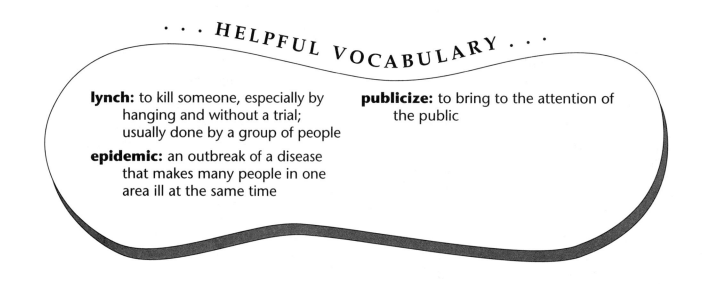

· · · HELPFUL VOCABULARY · · ·

lynch: to kill someone, especially by hanging and without a trial; usually done by a group of people

epidemic: an outbreak of a disease that makes many people in one area ill at the same time

publicize: to bring to the attention of the public

THINKING ABOUT WHAT YOU HAVE READ

1. Where was Wells born?

_____

_____

2. What important lesson did her parents teach her?

_____

_____

3. When she was fourteen, how did her life change?

_____

_____

_____

4. Why did Wells start writing articles for the newspapers in Memphis?

_____

_____

_____

5. What caused Wells to begin looking into lynching?

_____

_____

_____

6. Why do you think no one would talk about lynching?

_____

_____

7. Why was Wells such a great reporter and newspaper publisher?

_____

_____

8. Who are some other African Americans who fought for people's rights?

_____

_____

_____

WORKING WITH WORDS

A **prefix** is a letter or group of letters that we place at the beginning of a word or word root to change the meaning. The prefix *un-* means "not" or "opposite."

Example: *unfair.* Ida Wells quickly realized that African Americans often received *unfair* treatment.

List three words and then make new words by adding the prefix *un-*.

pack   **unpack**

_____   _____

_____   _____

_____   _____

The prefix *re-* means "back" or "again." List three words and then make new words by adding the prefix *re-*.

pay   **repay**

_____   _____

_____   _____

_____   _____

Look at the words in bold print. Then look at the pairs of words below them. The words in bold explain the relationship between the pair of words that follows. Can you write three more pairs of words for each grouping?

opposites   **whole to part**

first—last   cup—handle

_____   _____

_____   _____

_____   _____

locations	**part to whole**
Holly Springs—Mississippi	page—newspaper
_____	_____
_____	_____
_____	_____

An **idiom** is a group of words that have a special meaning. If you do not know the special meaning, you will not understand what a person is saying. In fact, it may sound very silly. For example, "It was raining cats and dogs." Read the explanations of the following idioms. Then write your own sentence using the idiom.

The idiom "a chip off the old block" means that a child looks or acts like one of his or her parents. When Ida B. Wells started to fight for a better life for all African Americans, many people said she was a chip off the old block.

_____

_____

_____

The idiom "butterflies in the stomach" means a strange feeling caused by fear or nervousness. Look again at the story. Ida B. Wells must have had butterflies in her stomach when she started to investigate the lynchings of her friends.

_____

_____

_____

WRITING SKILLS

Write a paragraph about a time when you or someone you know did something that was brave. Be sure that your paragraph has a topic sentence, which gives the main idea of the paragraph, and a concluding sentence, which lets the reader know that you have finished your discussion.

First, write down some key ideas. When you have finished your paragraph, proofread your writing. Check it for correct spelling, grammar, capitalization, and punctuation.

Key ideas:

_____

_____

_____

Paragraph

_____

_____

_____

_____

_____

_____

_____

_____

Pretend you are doing the advertising for a lecture that Ida B. Wells is giving. Write a paragraph about Wells's life, which will be handed out at the event. Be sure that your paragraph has a topic sentence, which gives the main idea of the paragraph, and a concluding sentence, which lets the reader know that you have finished your discussion.

First, write down some key ideas. When you have finished your paragraph, proofread your writing. Check it for correct spelling, grammar, capitalization, and punctuation. When you have finished, make a poster telling about the lecture.

Key ideas:

_____

_____

_____

The Life of Ida B. Wells

_____

_____

_____

_____

_____

_____

_____

_____

_____

_____

_____

_____

Poster

_____

_____

Bettman/Corbis

Janet Guthrie
1938–

Janet Guthrie was a pioneer in auto racing. Only a few years before she began racing at the Indianapolis 500, auto racing's top event, women were not even allowed to enter the area where cars were repaired and refueled. She worked her way through different levels of auto racing to achieve a remarkable record and to become the first woman to compete in the Indy 500.

Guthrie was born in Iowa City, Iowa, the oldest of five children. Her father, who was a commercial pilot, moved the family to Miami, Florida, when Janet was three. Guthrie's adventurous spirit showed up early. At the age of thirteen, she was flying a small Piper Cub plane; by the time she was sixteen, she had made a parachute jump and was flying solo.

Guthrie earned a private pilot's license at seventeen, got a commercial flying license at nineteen, and qualified as an instructor two years later.

When asked "Why do you think you were so daring?," Guthrie replied, "I have an adventuresome nature, and I had the good fortune to have parents who didn't say I couldn't do this or that because I was a girl." She also says that as a child she was very influenced by the books she borrowed from the library. "I loved reading adventure stories where the heroes, mostly boys, were always running off to sea, having wonderful adventures. I'd imagine myself in their place."

After earning a degree in physics from the University of Michigan in 1960, she worked as an aerospace engineer on Long Island. The United States space exploration program was just beginning; her job was to help develop vehicles to be used in space.

That same year Guthrie bought her first sports car, a used Jaguar XK 120. She joined a sports-car club and loved competing both on zigzag courses called gymkhanas and in higher-speed events known as hill climbs. Within two years, she had her first sports-car racing license.

In 1963, Guthrie bought a used Jaguar XK 140 and started entering sports-car races. In 1964, she taught herself how to rebuild the engine. Then she finished second in her class and seventh overall in the six-hour, 500-mile race at Watkins Glen, New York, while competing against much more powerful cars.

Soon Guthrie was entering more advanced races. In order to concentrate full time on auto racing, she quit her job. By 1971, she had **logged** nine straight finishes in the nation's top sports-car **endurance** events. Her record was excellent, and she wanted to race professionally, full-time. But no team owners wanted a woman racing driver.

Guthrie decided to build her own race car. She bought a Toyota Celica and rebuilt it. But it took a year until it was in racing shape, and by the time it was finished the racing series had been canceled. She was extremely disappointed, but Guthrie did not quit. She found a sponsor and raced her car in amateur events. Even though she worked part-time, by the end of 1975, Guthrie was deep in debt, and her car was out-of-date.

In 1976, a car designer and builder, Rolla Vollstedt, offered her one of his cars to race in the Indianapolis 500. Drivers, fans, and many other people connected with this race objected to having a woman driver participate. Using Vollstedt's car, Guthrie passed the rookie test but later was forced to withdraw because of mechanical problems. However, the defending champion, A. J. Foyt, let her take his backup car out in practice, so that she could show how good she was. Guthrie easily topped 181 mph, the speed needed to **qualify.** But Foyt did not want her to drive his car in the actual race, so she missed her chance to compete at the Indy 500 that year.

The following year Rolla Vollstedt bought a new car for Guthrie, and she returned to Indianapolis. On her first day out, during a time trial, she **posted** the highest speed of any driver. She qualified easily with a four-lap average speed of 188.402 mph in a field of thirty-three cars. When the race started, she had high hopes. For the first few laps, everything went well, but suddenly there was a mysterious engine problem. While the crew tried to repair it, fuel leaked into the cockpit and soaked through Guthrie's driving outfit, burning her. Every time the crew thought the problem was fixed, she roared back on to the track. But eventually the car broke down, and she had to drop out of the race.

Guthrie knew that if she wanted to race at the Indy 500, she needed better equipment. Luckily, just a month before the 1978 race, an oil company agreed to sponsor her. She quickly formed her own racing team and qualified for the race in fifteenth place.

Then just two days before the race, Guthrie **fractured** her right wrist. She told no one about her injury. More than 400,000 fans saw Guthrie become the first woman to complete the Indianapolis 500. Finishing in ninth place, she defeated some of the world's best drivers. However, her performance was impressive for another reason. Because of her injured right wrist, Guthrie had to use her left hand to shift and to do most of the steering. With her victory, people could no longer say that women did not have the strength or ability to handle fast cars.

Years later, when asked why, despite so many setbacks, she never gave up, Guthrie replied, "Once I started racing, it seemed to me that's what I was born to do."

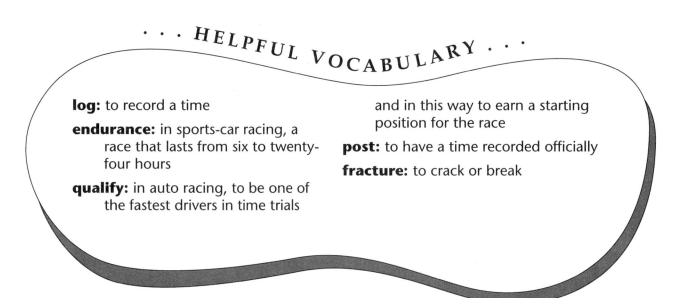

· · · HELPFUL VOCABULARY · · ·

log: to record a time

endurance: in sports-car racing, a race that lasts from six to twenty-four hours

qualify: in auto racing, to be one of the fastest drivers in time trials and in this way to earn a starting position for the race

post: to have a time recorded officially

fracture: to crack or break

THINKING ABOUT WHAT YOU HAVE READ

1. How was Janet Guthrie a pioneer in auto racing?

_____

_____

2. What are some of the unusual things Guthrie did as a teenager?

_____

_____

_____

3. Why does Guthrie think she was such a daring child and teenager?

_____

_____

_____

4. What did she study at college?

_____

5. Why do you think most sponsors and owners objected to a woman driver?

_____

_____

_____

6. Why was Rolla Vollstedt an important person in Guthrie's life?

_____

_____

7. Why do you think the oil company agreed to sponsor Guthrie in 1978?

_____

_____

_____

8. Why was Janet's performance at the 1978 Indianapolis 500 race so
   amazing?

   _____

   _____

   _____

WORKING WITH WORDS

A **synonym** is a word that has the same or almost the same meaning as another word. *Cost* and *price* are synonyms. Think of synonyms for the words that follow. See if you can write two. Give yourself a bonus point if you can do the last one.

top   _____   _____

allow   _____   _____

start   _____   _____

amazing   _____   _____

repair   _____   _____

searching   _____   _____

mysterious   _____   _____

victory   _____   _____

A **proverb** is a short saying that expresses something that many people believe to be true. "All that glitters is not gold" is a proverb. It means that just because something looks good, it does not mean that it is good.

Explain how Janet Guthrie's racing career is an example of the proverb "If at first you don't succeed, try, try again."

_____

_____

Explain how Guthrie's career is an example of the proverb "The apple doesn't fall far from the tree."

_____

_____

Look at the words *table* and *sofa*. They belong to the same general class or group. Both are pieces of furniture. They differ from each other in that you sit at one and you sit on the other. Now look at the following pairs of words. Write down what class or group they belong to. Then write one way in which they are different. Give yourself a bonus point if you can do the last one.

sports car—station wagon

_____

_____

helmet—goggles

_____

_____

speedometer—fuel gauge

_____

_____

Piper Cub plane—jet

_____

_____

WRITING SKILLS

Pretend that you are Janet Guthrie. It is 1978, the night after your first race in the Indy 500. You are writing in your diary. What are your feelings and thoughts?

First, write down some key ideas. When you have finished your paragraph, proofread your writing. Check it for correct spelling, grammar, capitalization, and punctuation.

Key ideas:

_____

_____

_____

Paragraph

_____

_____

_____

_____

_____

_____

_____

_____

Janet Guthrie says, "Once I started racing, it seemed to me that's what I was born to do." What do you think you are born to do? Write a paragraph about it.

Before you write the paragraph, write down some key ideas. When you have finished your paragraph, proofread your writing. Check it for correct spelling, grammar, capitalization, and punctuation.

Key ideas:

_____

_____

_____

Paragraph

_____

_____

_____

_____

_____

_____

_____

_____

_____

If you worked on a ship, where you would you like it to travel?

_____

_____

Courtesy of Sheridan House, publisher, *Titanic Survivor*, edited by John Maxton-Graham, 1997

Violet Jessop
1887–1971

Many people have heard of the great ship *Titanic,* which sank in 1912 on her first voyage with a loss of l,513 lives. Too few people, however, know the story of Violet Jessop, a young stewardess on this **legendary** ship. Jessop not only lived through the *Titanic* disaster, but four years later she survived the sinking of another great British ship, the *Brittanic.*

Jessop was born in Argentina where her parents had moved from Ireland. She was the oldest of six children in a family that was very close. As a child she was often sick. But from an early age, because her parents were poor, she helped her mother with the cooking and housecleaning.

After her father died, the family moved to England. To support them, her mother took a job as a stewardess on a ship. Jessop, who was sixteen, and her brothers and sister were sent to boarding schools. Several years later, when her mother got sick and was advised to return home to rest, the family no longer had money to live on. To help them, Jessop found a job as a ship stewardess. Besides her pay from the shipping company, she would receive tips from the passengers.

Jessop worked in the hotel department of the ship. Her job was to look after a group of passengers and their cabins. She brought the passengers their breakfast and tea trays, answered their calls, ran errands for them, and kept their cabins clean. Jessop wrote that after a day of work, "my shoes felt full of feet and life seemed one big ache."

Although she was often homesick and worried about her family, she was glad she could send them the money they needed. In addition, Jessop discovered that she loved traveling. She made good friends among the crew. At the end of each voyage, she was back in England, where she could see her family.

In 1912, the *Titanic*, the largest cruise ship yet built, would make its first trip. The shipping company that Jessop worked for began choosing the very best stewards and stewardesses to work on this luxury ship. Jessop was delighted when she was chosen.

On the night the ship hit the iceberg, Jessop had finished her work and was comfortably in bed reading magazines. She was almost ready to fall asleep when there was a great crash. Then the sound of the engines stopped. Jessop, who had always been afraid of a ship sinking, lay in bed. One of the stewards came to her room to tell her that the ship was sinking.

Jessop quickly got up and went to look after her passengers. She helped people fix lifebelts and reminded them to put on warm clothing and to take blankets and valuables. She returned to her room to gather some of her things together. Then she headed back to the deck, where the lifeboats were being filled with women and children.

Besides the luxury passengers, the *Titanic* was also carrying many poor people, who were leaving their countries to find a better life in the United States. Because many of these immigrants did not speak English, they did not understand what they were told to do. An officer asked Jessop to get into a lifeboat, hoping that these passengers would follow her example. When she was in the boat, the officer called, "Look after this, will you?" She reached out and received a baby wrapped in a blanket. Soon the lifeboat pulled away from the ship; Jessop watched stunned as the mighty *Titanic* sank.

The following day, Jessop's small boat was spotted by the *Carpathia*. When she got on board, the baby's mother rushed up to her, snatched her child, and moved quickly away. Jessop never saw them again. The *Carpathia* brought all the survivors to New York.

Jessop needed her salary to support her family. Realizing that she would have to return to her sea life quickly or she would become afraid, she took another job as stewardess.

Two years later, when World War I broke out, Jessop decided to volunteer as a nurse. Following a brief training, she began working on the *Brittanic*, a **sister ship** of the *Titanic*, which was serving as a British hospital ship. On November 21, 1916, while people on the *Brittanic* were eating breakfast, they heard a sudden, dull, deafening roar. A German **mine** had struck the ship. Jessop made her way to her cabin to gather things to take with her in the lifeboat. She quickly collected what was dearest to her, along with her toothbrush. She remembered that in the days after being rescued from the *Titanic*, she had been unable to find a single toothbrush.

With many others, she climbed into the lifeboat and was lowered into the ocean. But it had barely touched the water when Jessop saw all of the other passengers jump out. Looking about her, she saw the boat being pulled toward the ship's propellers, which were chopping up everything near them. She had never learned to swim and had always been afraid of drowning. But suddenly she found she was no longer afraid. With no time to waste, she **plunged** into the ocean and went under.

As she rose to the surface, something struck her forcefully on the back of her head and gashed her leg. Luckily, a motorboat from the ship came to rescue the people in the water who were still alive. Twenty-eight people had been killed. Jessop's leg took three years to heal. For a long time after the rescue, her head hurt terribly, but she never told anyone. Not until years later did she discover that her skull had been badly fractured.

When the war ended in 1918, Jessop worked again as a stewardess, sailing on five world cruises. She was delighted to visit so many places she had always wanted to see. Later she worked as a clerk in an office and in a wallpaper factory. When Jessop was sixty-one years old, she signed up for a two-year job on ships going to South America. After she finally retired from the sea, she moved to a small cottage in England where she became an enthusiastic gardener.

Following her death, a shipmate wrote, "She had given so much comfort and care to so many during her lifetime. . . . She was so like a mother to us younger members of the ship's company. . . . During the daily inspections at sea, the captain or the officers would always have a few words with Violet. . . . She was a remarkable woman who loved the sea and ships."

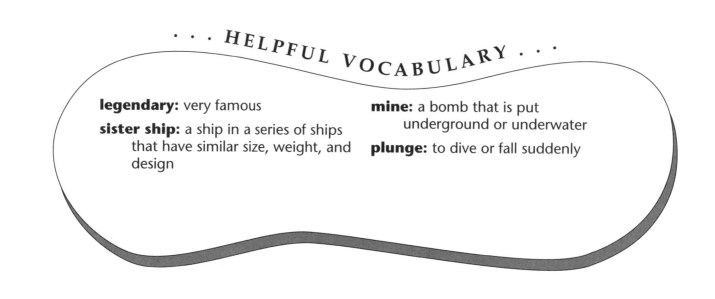

· · · HELPFUL VOCABULARY · · ·

legendary: very famous

sister ship: a ship in a series of ships that have similar size, weight, and design

mine: a bomb that is put underground or underwater

plunge: to dive or fall suddenly

THINKING ABOUT WHAT YOU HAVE READ

1. Why did Jessop start working as a stewardess?

_____

_____

2. What kinds of things did a stewardess do?

_____

_____

_____

3. When she was a stewardess, what were the two things Jessop feared?

_____

_____

_____

4. What did she do when she learned the *Titanic* was sinking?

_____

_____

_____

5. Why do you think people were so surprised when the *Titanic* sank?

_____

_____

_____

6. How do you think Jessop's job compares to a stewardess's job on an airplane today?

_____

_____

7. What are two examples of Jessop's bravery?

_____

_____

8. Why do you think Jessop signed up as a stewardess when she was sixty-one years old?

_____

_____

_____

WORKING WITH WORDS

Sometimes words have more than one meaning. In the following sentences, the word in bold print has one meaning. Write what it is. Then write another meaning the word may have. Give yourself a bonus point if you can do the last one.

Example: I **beat** three eggs to make an omelet. In the sentence, *beat* means to stir or mix. *Beat* can also mean to hit again and again.

Many people have heard of the **great** ship *Titanic.*

_____

_____

From an **early** age she helped her mother with the cooking.

_____

_____

She made some **good** friends among the crew.

_____

_____

Jessop heard a **dull,** deafening roar.

_____

_____

She would get **tips** from the passengers.

_____

_____

An **antonym** is a word that has the opposite meaning of another word. *Cruel* is an antonym of *kind*. Write an antonym for each of these words.

sink _____   always _____

few _____   cease _____

sickly _____   quickly _____

glad _____   find _____

A **simile** is a phrase or expression introduced by the words *like* or *as;* it compares two things that are not alike. For example, Jessop must have been *as nervous as a cat* when the *Titanic* sank. See if you can use this simile in a sentence.

_____

_____

Now explain what these similes mean and use them in sentences. Give yourself a bonus point if you can do the last one.

Helping the passengers, she was *as cool as a cucumber.*

_____

_____

_____

Sitting in the lifeboat, she was *as cold as ice.*

_____

_____

_____

When she was rescued, she looked *as white as a sheet.*

_____

_____

_____

WRITING SKILLS

An **expanded paragraph** is a full-length paragraph that lets you give as much information as you like about each one of your supporting ideas. So that your meaning is clear, you should separate your supporting ideas with transitions. A **transition word** gives the reader the signal that you have finished discussing one idea and are ready to move to the next idea. These are common transition words.

first   second   next   last   finally

A shipmate said that Violet Jessop was a remarkable woman. What do you think? Write an expanded paragraph that uses examples from the story for supporting ideas. Try to use at least three of the transition words above. Be sure that your paragraph has a topic sentence, which gives the main idea of the paragraph, and a concluding sentence, which lets the reader know that you have finished your discussion.

First, write down some key ideas. When you have finished your paragraph, proofread your writing. Check it for correct spelling, grammar, capitalization, and punctuation.

Key ideas:

_____

_____

_____

_____

Paragraph

_____

_____

_____

_____

_____

_____

_____

_____

_____

_____

Pretend you work for an employment agency and have to advertise for a stewardess's job. List three reasons people would want the job. Next list three skills people need to have. Then write your ad. Be sure to proofread it.

_____   _____   _____

_____   _____   _____

Advertisement

_____

_____

_____

_____

_____

_____

_____

_____

What are some of the things that a theater director does?

_____

_____

Photo by Ms. J. Maloof

George C. Wolfe
1954–

George Wolfe, a well-known playwright and theater director, says that a trip to New York City, the summer before his thirteenth birthday, changed his life. He had traveled with his mother from their home in Frankfort, Kentucky, to New York City, so that his mother could study at New York University. While staying in New York, George saw a play that completely enchanted him. Wolfe says that when he saw *West Side Story*, he was, "totally **transformed.**" He realized that on stage you could show things in a way that you could not do anywhere else. He remembered, "It was like something popped in my brain." Later, in his own directing career, Wolfe became known for trying new and different things.

He was not always so sure of himself, however. Wolfe grew up in a **segregated** community. He recalls that he could not see the movie *101 Dalmatians* because African-American children were not allowed into the local movie theater. At first, segregation did not make him less confident. Wolfe went to an African-American elementary school where his mother was principal. The grown-ups around him were always talking about the wonderful things African Americans had done. He remembers people telling him, his sister, and his two brothers, "This black person invented the light bulb; this black person invented the traffic light; this person did this; this person did that." So whenever Wolfe was insulted because he was an African American, it did not hurt as much because he had a strong sense of what African Americans had achieved.

Later, his family moved to a mostly white neighborhood where he attended a large **integrated** high school. With only a few African Americans in the school, Wolfe found it very hard to adjust and spent a lot of time by himself. He says, "I started reading encyclopedia volumes as if they were comic books, and I became fascinated with Greek mythology. The gods became friends of mine." Wolfe developed a **stutter** and avoided the drama department at school. Although he was interested in acting, he thought that he "was too awkward and weird." Looking back, he says that he didn't have the confidence to act.

The following summer, Wolfe went with his mother to Miami University in Oxford, Ohio, where she was working on her doctorate. His mother enrolled him in a theater program, which he loved. He worked twelve to fourteen hours a day, and his stutter disappeared. Wolfe says it was then that he decided to make the theater his life. When Wolfe returned to high school, he was a different person. He became the most active member of the drama department.

Wolfe went to college in California. The plays he read and saw about African Americans did not interest him, so he started writing his own plays. In 1979, after graduation, he moved to New York City where he continued his training in theater. He started having his plays produced.

Wolfe's first play that opened in New York was a total failure. A critic wrote, "The best directing the director could have done was put a sign on the door saying 'Do Not Enter!',", but Wolfe didn't give up. When his next play, *The Colored Museum*, was staged in New Jersey, Joseph Papp saw it. He was the director of the New York Shakespeare Festival and was famous for the plays he produced. Papp was so impressed that he quickly decided to present it in New York City. The play was very successful, and soon Wolfe was chosen to be a director at the Public Theater, which is part of the New York Shakespeare Festival.

Meanwhile, Wolfe was busy writing the words for a musical that would be called *Jelly's Last Jam.* It told the story of the life of Jelly Roll Morton, an early twentieth-century jazz musician, who was a pioneer in jazz. The play was a great triumph.

In 1993, two years after Joseph Papp's death, Wolfe was appointed director of the theater that Papp had begun. Wolfe was delighted with his new job. He would have full control over what the theater produced. He was eager to continue the work of this theater, which had been to entertain and educate the public.

Then only a few years later, disaster struck. His mother died of heart disease. His house burned down, and he lost almost everything he owned. His doctor told him that one of his kidneys no longer worked.

For a year, simply to stay alive, Wolfe had to go three times a week to a clinic to be hooked up to a machine that cleaned **toxins** from his body. Very few people knew he was ill. During this time, Wolfe ran his theater and directed three plays. He says that his mother taught him to "keep going no matter what."

Luckily, he was able to receive a kidney transplant. His brother William gave him one of his kidneys. Now Wolfe is fully recovered. He is happy to be alive and loves his job. He says, "When you direct, you sculpt and shape the action around you."

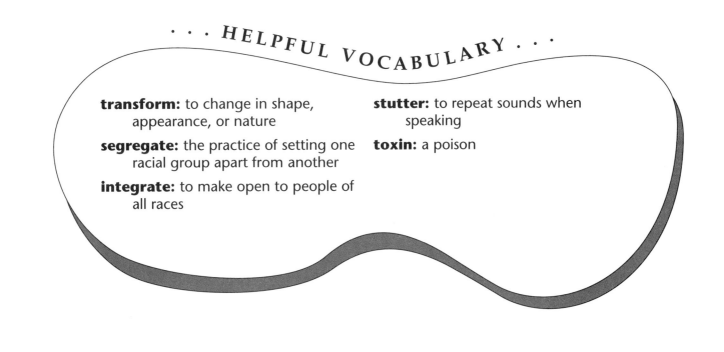

· · · HELPFUL VOCABULARY · · ·

transform: to change in shape, appearance, or nature

segregate: the practice of setting one racial group apart from another

integrate: to make open to people of all races

stutter: to repeat sounds when speaking

toxin: a poison

THINKING ABOUT WHAT YOU HAVE READ

1. When George Wolfe was a boy, what event changed his life?

_____

_____

2. How do you think Wolfe felt when he could not see *101 Dalmatians?*

_____

_____

_____

3. How did he change when he went to high school?

_____

_____

_____

4. In what ways did Wolfe's mother help him?

_____

_____

_____

5. When did Wolfe stop stuttering?

_____

_____

_____

6. Why was Joseph Papp a great help to George Wolfe?

_____

_____

7. Why do you think Wolfe wanted to write a play about Jelly Roll Morton?

_____

_____

8. Why do you think Wolfe was able to face all the terrible things that happened to him?

_____

_____

_____

WORKING WITH WORDS

When George Wolfe saw the play *West Side Story,* he thought it was marvelous. Think of a play or movie you have liked. Write down its name and then list as many describing words as you can that tell what it was like. Try to think of at least four.

Name of play or movie: _____

_____   _____   _____

_____   _____   _____

Some words sound alike but are spelled differently and have different meanings. These words are called **homophones.**

Example: *where* and *wear.* George Wolfe moved to New York City, *where* he continued studying theater. What did you *wear* to the play?

See if you can fill in the blanks with homophones. Be sure to read both sentences in the pair before you write your answers. Give yourself a bonus point if you can do the last two.

The idea for the play came from a _____ story.

I want a new fishing rod and _____ for my birthday.

George spent his _____ allowance on theater tickets.

I had a _____ in my sock, so I threw it away.

The play was so good that I was never _____.

A _____ in the floor of the stage cracked.

Which play did your class _____ to put on for Thanksgiving?

The little girl _____ her food carefully.

I started to _____ when I saw the terrible play.

My brother has _____ three inches this year!

The actor walked down the _____ of the theater.

_____ meet you after the play.

The _____ actor usually has to wear a wig.

The sick baby _____ all night.

In an **analogy,** you are trying to figure out the connection between two pairs of words. Example: playwright is to play as poet is to _____.

First, you must understand the connection between the words in the first pair, playwright/play. Make a picture in your mind of these words. Think how they are related. Then make a sentence describing what you see.

A playwright *writes* a play.

Now use the word you have pictured to make the same connection between the second pair of words. What does a poet write?

A poet *writes* a poem.

The analogy, then, is playwright is to play as poet is to poem.

In the following analogies, decide what the connection is between the first pair of words. Make a picture of these words in your mind. Think how they are related. Next, write a word in the blank that will show the same connection between the second pair of words.

George Wolfe is to playwright as Babe Ruth is to _____.

Well-known is to famous as sleepy is to _____.

Theater is to play as stadium is to _____.

Titanic is to movie as *Harry Potter and the Sorcerer's Stone* is to _____.

Kentucky is to Nevada as Mexico is to _____.

Principal is to school as director is to _____.

WRITING SKILLS

Describe a trip you took one summer. What do you remember about it? Were you excited or nervous?

Be sure that your paragraph has a topic sentence, which gives the main idea of the paragraph, and a concluding sentence, which lets the reader know that you have finished your discussion.

First, write down some key ideas. When you have finished your paragraph, proofread your writing. Check it for correct spelling, grammar, capitalization, and punctuation.

Key ideas:

_____

_____

_____

Paragraph

_____

_____

_____

_____

_____

_____

_____

George's first play in New York was a failure, but he did not give up. Write about a time you had difficulties but did not give up. First, write down some key ideas. When you have finished your paragraph, proof-read your writing. Check it for correct spelling, grammar, capitalization, and punctuation.

Key ideas:

_____

_____

_____

Paragraph

_____

_____

_____

_____

_____

_____

_____

_____

_____

_____

What does a person need to become an outstanding athlete?

Photo by Russ Adams

Rosemary Casals
1948–

Rosemary Casals won more than ninety tennis tournaments, including five Wimbledon doubles titles. She is considered one of the best doubles players in the history of the game. Throughout her tennis career she fought hard to make important changes in the tennis world.

Casals was born in San Francisco, California, to a poor family who had emigrated from El Salvador. When she was only a year old, her parents decided that they could not afford to take care of her and her older sister. So her great aunt and uncle, Maria and Manuel Casals, who had also come from El Salvador, raised the two sisters. Manuel Casals, a **former** member of El Salvador's national soccer team, taught eight-year-old

Casals to play tennis at a public park in San Francisco. Her uncle was the only tennis coach she would ever have. By the time she was nine, Casals was competing in **local** tennis tournaments.

Her background was different from most of the other players. In those days, tennis was generally played at expensive country clubs, whose members were often wealthy white people. Casals's aunt and uncle could not afford the best equipment or clothes; often she was ignored by other players. At one junior event, ten-year-old Casals had to sleep for several nights in the old family car because the sponsor of the event did not provide a promised room. She said, "It was a rude awakening. The other kids had nice tennis clothes, nice rackets, nice white shoes and came in Cadillacs. I felt **stigmatized** because we were poor." But in spite of all of this, she won the trophy for the tournament.

At five feet two inches tall, Casals was well below the average height of a competitive woman player. This put her at a great disadvantage on the court. She would do anything to win a match, even trying a between-the-legs shot. To make up for her short height, she developed great speed, extremely fast reflexes, and a great variety of shots, including a fierce volley, lob, and smash.

By the time she was sixteen, Casals was competing nationally, and a year later she was ranked eleventh in the country. She explained, "I wanted to be someone. I knew I was good, and winning tournaments— it's a kind of way of being accepted."

She teamed up with Billie Jean King in doubles, and soon they were unbeatable. With their furious and appealing playing style, they attracted new spectators, the **media,** and sponsors to women's tennis games.

In 1968, for the first time, amateur and professional tennis players were allowed to compete against each other for prize money. Casals became one of the first women to tour as a professional. However, female tennis players were earning much less than male tennis players. In 1970, before the Pacific Southwest Open, Casals, along with other women players, protested that as always the men players would receive much more money than the women players. The United States Lawn Tennis Association, which ran all of the tournaments, ignored them.

Many of the women players decided to organize a women's tournament, the Virginia Slims Invitational. They set it for the same time as the Pacific Southwest Open. Casals with six other United States women tennis players **boycotted** the Pacific Southwest Open so that they could play in the Virginia Slims Invitational. Casals said, "I go through the same headaches trying to live and play tennis as the men do. I'm for equal pay for equal play." She won the first prize, which was $1,600, and from 1970 to 1978 she would win eight more Virginia Slims titles.

In the mid 1970s, besides playing in regular tennis tournaments, she played for several professional women's teams, including the Detroit Loves and the Oakland Breakland. She also coached the Los Angeles Strings. The busy playing schedule led to an injury to her knee; after knee surgery in 1978, she played fewer tournaments.

In 1981, Casals started a company that acted as an agency for new tennis players and that promoted a Women's Classic Tour. She also set up her own television company. Now, in her spare time Casals enjoys playing golf as well as tennis.

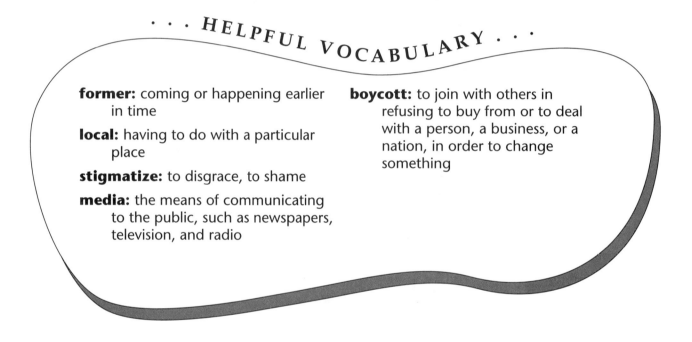

· · · HELPFUL VOCABULARY · · ·

former: coming or happening earlier in time

local: having to do with a particular place

stigmatize: to disgrace, to shame

media: the means of communicating to the public, such as newspapers, television, and radio

boycott: to join with others in refusing to buy from or to deal with a person, a business, or a nation, in order to change something

THINKING ABOUT WHAT YOU HAVE READ

1. Who was the most important person in Rosemary Casals's tennis career?

_____

_____

2. How old was Casals when she started playing in local tennis contests?

_____

_____

_____

3. How was her background different from other young tennis players?

_____

_____

_____

4. How did Casals make up for her short height?

_____

_____

_____

5. Why do you think she always worked so hard to improve her tennis game?

_____

_____

_____

6. How did Casals make women's tennis more popular with fans?

_____

_____

7. How did Casals change tennis for women players?

_____

_____

8. Why do you think Casals played doubles games?

_____

_____

_____

WORKING WITH WORDS

List the items that tennis players need when they play outdoors. Try to think of four. Give yourself a bonus point if you can think of more than four.

_____   _____   _____

_____   _____   _____

Look at the words *macaroni* and *spaghetti*. They belong to the same general class or group. Both are a kind of pasta. They differ from each other in that one is short and hollow and the other is long and thin. Now look at the following pairs of words. Write down what class or group they belong to. Then write one way in which they are different. Give yourself a bonus point if you can do the last two.

sneakers—slippers

_____

_____

racket—hockey stick

_____

_____

tennis ball—basketball

_____

_____

pitcher—quarterback

_____

_____

_____

tennis hat—football helmet

_____

_____

_____

A **synonym** is a word that has the same or almost the same meaning as another word. *Small* and *little* are synonyms. Think of synonyms for the words that follow. See if you can write two.

tournament   _____   _____

wealthy   _____   _____

organize   _____   _____

great   _____   _____

fast   _____   _____

split   _____   _____

ignored   _____   _____

provided   _____   _____

WRITING SKILLS

Rosemary Casals had to work hard to become a great tennis player. Tell about a time you had to work hard to do something.

_____

_____

_____

_____

_____

_____

_____

Write a paragraph about Rosemary Casals's life. Be sure that your paragraph has a topic sentence, which gives the main idea of the paragraph, and a concluding sentence, which lets the reader know that you have finished your discussion.

First, write down some key ideas. When you have finished your paragraph, proofread your writing. Check it for correct spelling, grammar, capitalization, and punctuation.

Key ideas:

_____

_____

_____

Paragraph

_____

_____

_____

Courtesy of Madame Tussaud's, London

Marie Grosholtz Tussaud
1761–1850

Each year millions of people visit Madame Tussaud's Wax Museum in London; they are amazed by the lifelike wax figures they see displayed. But few of these visitors know the remarkable story of the museum's founder, Marie Grosholtz Tussaud. At a time when few women worked outside of their homes, Tussaud not only had her own business but made it very successful. By combining entertainment with history, her wax museum gave and continues to give pleasure and knowledge to many people.

Tussaud was born in Strasbourg, France. Because her father died before her birth, Tussaud's mother had to find work. She took a job as a housekeeper and cook for a **physician** in Bern, Switzerland, Dr. Philippe

Curtius. In addition to his work as a doctor, he was known for the small sculptures he made in wax. At that time, small wax **busts** were very popular, so Dr. Curtius started a small waxwork museum in Bern. In 1763, he traveled to Paris, France, to set up another museum. After he arrived, so many important people wanted him to sculpt a portrait of their head in wax that he decided to stay in Paris. He sent for his housekeeper and her daughter to join him.

Tussaud was a bright and lively child. Dr. Curtius, who had no children of his own, liked her. When she was six years old, Dr. Curtius said that she could be his student. She watched everything he did, and by the time she was a teenager, she was a good sculptress. Her goal was to make perfect wax models. Tussaud's work was so skillful and accurate that by the time she was seventeen, Dr. Curtius allowed her to model heads of the famous people who came to his studio.

One of these was Princess Elizabeth, the sister of King Louis XVI of France. During a visit to Dr. Curtius, the princess noticed Tussaud's work and was impressed with the way she shaped a face. Soon after, the princess appointed the twenty-year-old Tussaud to be art tutor at Versailles, the home of the king of France. Tussaud worked there for eight years, meeting many important people in the French court.

In 1789, however, Dr. Curtius asked her to return to Paris. The French Revolution to **overthrow** the king had just begun; it was not safe to be working for the king's family. Dr. Curtius continued working in his studio. He began adding wax portraits of the leaders of the revolution to his museum. During this time, many people were killed. Tussaud was ordered by the new government to make **death masks** of many of them.

In 1792, Dr. Curtius died and left Marie Tussaud everything he owned. Over the next several years, she married, had two sons, and worked hard making models of famous people.

By the early 1800s, however, wax portraits were no longer popular in Paris. Suddenly, Tussaud did not have much work. She was looking for new ideas when an old friend suggested that she bring a collection of wax portraits to London for an exhibition. Tussaud thought this was a good idea and traveled to London.

The show was a great success. People enjoyed looking at Tussaud's life-sized wax figures of well-known people from French history. The models were beautifully displayed with dramatic lighting. The clothes for each figure were copied perfectly.

Tussaud knew that to make money she would always need new audiences. She decided to travel through the country, taking the exhibition with her. For four years she toured Scotland and Ireland. In 1808,

Tussaud returned to London; then for the next twenty-six years, she toured England, visiting seventy-five towns and small villages.

Tussaud never allowed her exhibits to become outdated or boring. She was always adding figures of famous leaders and well-known criminals that people were talking about. Whenever there was an important event, such as the crowning of a queen or king of England, she made wax figures or wax scenes.

Once, when some men tried to kill King George III of England, Tussaud made an excellent wax figure of one of them. Then using the wax figure, Tussaud set up a scary scene to show the men trying to kill the king. People came to stare at, shiver over, and be scared by what they saw. Tussaud had started a fashion, the room of horrors.

When Tussaud was seventy-five years old, she set up a permanent exhibition in London. By then she did not use life masks; she created her figures directly in wax, using personal observation, just as a sculptor does.

Even though her health got worse as she grew older, Marie Tussaud still came to the exhibition nearly every day. Today, among the many wax figures at the museum, visitors see a small old lady dressed in black. This is Madame Tussaud's portrait of herself, modeled when she was eighty-one years old.

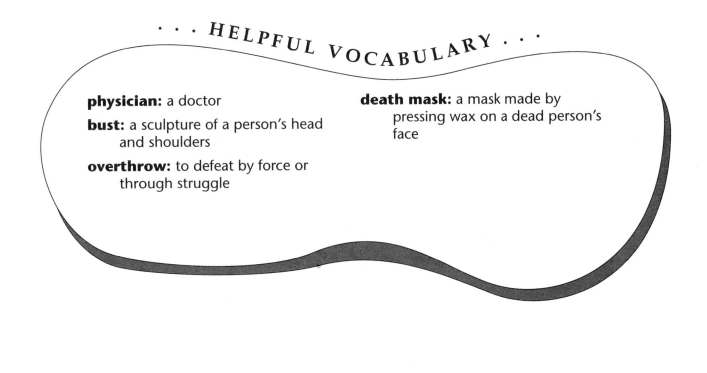

· · · HELPFUL VOCABULARY · · ·

physician: a doctor

bust: a sculpture of a person's head and shoulders

overthrow: to defeat by force or through struggle

death mask: a mask made by pressing wax on a dead person's face

THINKING ABOUT WHAT YOU HAVE READ

1. What do people find so surprising at Madame Tussaud's Wax Museum?

_____

_____

2. When Marie Tussaud was living, why do you think there were not many successful businesswomen?

_____

_____

_____

3. Why was Dr. Curtius such an important person in Tussaud's life?

_____

_____

_____

4. Why was Tussaud such a fine sculptress?

_____

_____

_____

5. Why did English people enjoy Tussaud's wax figures?

_____

_____

6. Why did Tussaud start a room of horrors?

_____

_____

7. Why was she always going from town to town?

_____

_____

_____

8. Why do you think an elderly Marie Tussaud visited her exhibition almost daily?

_____

_____

_____

WORKING WITH WORDS

What three words did you learn from this story?

_____   _____   _____

Try to use two of them in sentences.

_____

_____

_____

A **suffix** is a letter or group of letters that we place at the end of a word or word root to change its meaning. The suffix -*able* means "possible to."

Example: *changeable*. Madame Tussaud wanted to *change* the figures in her exhibit. She wanted a *changeable* exhibit.

List three words and then make new words by adding the suffix -*able*.

read   **readable**

_____   _____

_____   _____

_____   _____

The suffix -*ly* means "like" or "manner of acting." List three words and then make new words by adding the suffix -*ly*.

live   **lively**

_____   _____

_____   _____

_____   _____

How are a hammer, a saw, a wrench, a screwdriver, and a pair of pliers alike? If you said they are all tools, you are correct. Now read the following sets of words and see if you can add two more items to each category. Write down how they are alike. Give yourself a bonus point if you can do the last one.

France   Switzerland   Germany

_____   _____

_____

brush   canvas   easel

_____   _____

_____

east   right   north

_____   _____

_____

tape   string   glue

_____   _____

_____

mermaid   Cinderella   unicorn

_____   _____

_____

WRITING SKILLS

An **expanded paragraph** is a full-length paragraph that lets you give as much information as you like about each one of your supporting ideas. So that your meaning is clear, you should separate your supporting ideas with transitions. A **transition word** gives the reader the signal that you have finished discussing one idea and are ready to move to the next idea. These are common transition words.

first   second   next   last   finally

If it were up to you, which three figures of famous people would you add to Madame Tussaud's Wax Museum? Write an expanded paragraph telling about these figures. Try to use at least three of the transition words above. Be sure that your paragraph has a topic sentence, which gives the main idea of the paragraph, and a concluding sentence, which lets the reader know that you have finished your discussion.

First, write down some key ideas. When you have finished your paragraph, proofread your writing. Check it for correct spelling, grammar, capitalization, and punctuation.

Key ideas:

_____

_____

_____

_____

Paragraph

_____

_____

_____

_____

_____

_____

_____

_____

_____

_____

_____

Imagine that you are visiting Madame Tussaud's Museum for the first time. What do you see? What do you like? Use details from the story for this. First, write down some key ideas. Be sure the paragraph has a topic and a concluding sentence. When you have finished, check your writing for correct spelling, grammar, capitalization, and punctuation.

Key ideas:

_____

_____

_____

Paragraph

_____

_____

_____

_____

_____

_____

_____

_____

_____

What are some animals you have taken care of?

Courtesy of Dr. William Karesh

William Karesh
1955–

    William Karesh is a veterinarian. However, the animals he takes care of through his work at the Wildlife **Convervation** Society are wild and live all over the world. He says this is the kind of job he has wanted to do since he was a child.

    Growing up in Charleston, South Carolina, Karesh dreamed of looking for unknown places and of caring for wild animals. He spent many hours exploring a neighboring lake and a nearby saltwater marsh and woods. Every spring he brought home orphaned blue jays, squirrels, and raccoons to raise. When they were old enough to return to the wild, Karesh designed and built cages, which used some of the bushes and trees in the yard. The cages looked like their natural homes. He always left the doors open so that the animals could leave at any time. But he also left food for them in case they wanted to come back.

Karesh remembers that when he was seven or eight, he was fascinated by Jim Fowler, one of the characters on the television program *Animal Kingdom.* He loved seeing Fowler work with animals, and in particular he remembers one episode when Fowler jumped from a helicopter and caught a twenty-foot long **anaconda** in a Venezuelan swamp. With the giant snake wrapped around him, Fowler disappeared under the spinning, muddy water a couple of times and finally wrestled the anaconda into obeying. Even though he did not know why Fowler was trying to control the snake, Karesh knew this was the kind of job he wanted to have. But then grown-ups explained that this job existed only on television.

By the time Karesh went to college, he no longer thought about working with animals. He studied different subjects but was not interested in any of them. Then a friend's mother reminded him of how happy he had been taking care of animals. Karesh realized this was the kind of job he should be training for.

In 1971, after he graduated from Clemson University with a degree in **zoology,** he became a zookeeper at the National Zoo in Washington, D.C. There he worked with large and dangerous animals. One of the scientists at the zoo advised him to go to veterinary school, because he would have a better chance of getting an interesting job. Karesh enrolled in veterinary school in Georgia. After graduation, he wanted to have experience working with as many **species** of animals as possible. So he took a job as a veterinarian at the famous San Diego Zoo and Wild Animal Park. Later, he became the director of a zoo in Seattle, Washington.

In 1989, Karesh was hired by the Wildlife Conservation Society of New York City to develop its "field veterinary program," the first of its kind in the world. His job was to provide medical help to animals in the wild and to give advice and training to local people and scientists who worked with wild animals.

With the help of workers in other countries, Karesh checks on the health of wild animals in places such as Argentina, Cameroon, and Indonesia. Together they examine the animals and collect hundreds of blood and tissue samples. The results of all these tests sometimes show conservation problems that have not yet been identified through other research methods. For example, he and his team discovered signs of **pesticide** in a group of sea birds on the rocky coast of Peru. This information can help the conservationists and government officials to create programs and laws to protect wildlife.

Karesh may also be called on to respond to a special crisis in an animal population. In Borneo, large forests were cut down to make farmland. The Indonesian Wildlife Department asked him to help move endangered orangutans, which were stranded in the small patches of remaining forest, to a nearby protected reserve.

Karesh has developed new uses of technology and these have had a big effect on conservation projects. Trying to lessen the dangers connected with getting blood and tissue samples from animals, he developed a special dart for fieldwork. The dart, which is fired at the animal with a dart gun, breaks the skin enough to pinch off a tiny piece of tissue before it falls back to the ground. Although it might take time later to find the dart, the method is much safer for both animals and humans. There is no need for a dangerous capture or the use of tranquilizing drugs. Now this dart has become a common tool for scientists and veterinarians who are gathering information on wild animals.

In the Democratic Republic of the Congo, Karesh used technology to help control the illegal killing of rhinos. After tranquilizing the animals with a drug, he drilled a tiny hole in their horns and put in small radio-tracking devices. Park managers then knew the location of individual animals and could protect them.

Over the years Karesh has worked with thousands of animals. He is often close to animals that can be dangerous. But he remains calm, has a steady aim with a dart gun, and, if all else fails, has excellent running and climbing skills.

Although his job is hard, uncomfortable, and sometimes dangerous, Karesh loves his work. He says, "Out in the wild I've seen the results of dedicated people pushing to make the planet a better place for all of us, plants and animals included. I know these people and they won't give up. They are ordinary human beings, like you and me, who have found their own way to contribute. They also know a secret: Each one of us can make a difference."

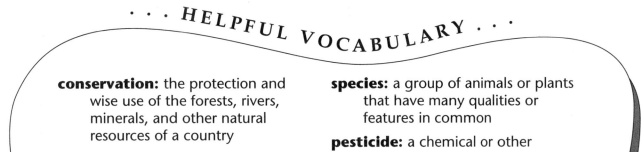

conservation: the protection and wise use of the forests, rivers, minerals, and other natural resources of a country

anaconda: a very large snake found in South America

zoology: the science that deals with the study of animals

species: a group of animals or plants that have many qualities or features in common

pesticide: a chemical or other substance that is used to destroy harmful plants or insects

THINKING ABOUT WHAT YOU HAVE READ

1. As a child, how did Karesh show he was interested in animals?

_____

_____

_____

2. Why do you think Karesh liked Jim Fowler's program so much?

_____

_____

3. Who were the two people whose advice greatly influenced Karesh
   when he was a young man?

_____

_____

4. What did the Wildlife Conservation Society hire Karesh to do?

_____

_____

5. Why is the dart that Karesh developed an improved method for getting
   blood and tissue samples from wild animals?

_____

_____

_____

6. Why are the radio-tracking devices in the rhinos horns so important for
   the park managers?

_____

_____

_____

7. Do you think Karesh's work is important? Explain your answer.

_____

_____

_____

8. Why do you think Karesh likes his job so much?

_____

_____

_____

9. Over the years, what has he learned that greatly helps him in his job?

_____

_____

_____

WORKING WITH WORDS

An **idiom** is a group of words that have a special meaning. If you do not know the special meaning, you will not understand what a person is saying. In fact, it may sound very silly. For example, "Don't let the cat out of the bag." Read the explanations of the following idioms. Then write your own sentence using the idiom. Give yourself a bonus point if you can do the last one.

The idiom "a close shave" means a narrow escape from danger. Sometimes, working with a tranquilizer gun, Karesh has had a close shave.

_____

_____

"Sitting on top of the world" means feeling very happy because of something you have accomplished. After Karesh helped move the orangutans to a safe place, he was sitting on top of the world.

_____

_____

The idiom "batting a thousand" means you are doing a perfect job. Many of the people who work with Karesh believe that he is batting a thousand now.

_____

_____

A **prefix** is a letter or group of letters that we place at the beginning of a word or word root to change the meaning. The prefix _in-_ means "in," "into," or "not."

Example: _inhuman._ Most people agree that being cruel to animals is _inhuman._

List three words and then make new words by adding the prefix *in-*.

complete   **incomplete**

_____   _____

_____   _____

_____   _____

The prefix *dis-* means "not" or "opposite of." List three words and then make new words by adding the prefix *dis-*.

believe   **disbelieve**

_____   _____

_____   _____

_____   _____

A **synonym** is a word that has the same or almost the same meaning as another word. *Happy* and *glad* are synonyms. Think of synonyms for the words that follow. See if you can write two. Give yourself a bonus point if you can do the last one.

help   _____   _____

kind   _____   _____

calm   _____   _____

dangerous   _____   _____

famous   _____   _____

excellent   _____   _____

discover   _____   _____

WRITING SKILLS

When Karesh was a boy, the television program *Animal Kingdom* had a big effect on him. What television program had a big effect on you? Why did you like it? What did you learn from it? Write a paragraph about this television program. Be sure that your paragraph has a topic sentence, which gives the main idea of the paragraph, and a concluding sentence, which lets the reader know that you have finished your discussion.

First, write down some key ideas. When you have finished your paragraph, proofread your writing. Check it for correct spelling, grammar, capitalization, and punctuation.

Key ideas:

_____

_____

_____

Paragraph

_____

_____

_____

_____

_____

_____

_____

_____

_____

Karesh has had many exciting experiences while working to help animals. If you were interviewing him for a television show, what are five questions you would like to ask him?

1. _____

2. _____

3. _____

4. _____

5. _____

Look at your questions. Think about what part of Karesh's life you find most interesting. Then write about it, explaining why you find it so fascinating. When you have finished your paragraph, proofread your writing. Check it for correct spelling, grammar, capitalization, and punctuation.

Paragraph

_____

_____

_____

_____

_____

_____

_____

_____

_____

_____

If you could have two completely different careers, what would they be?

_____

_____

Fannie Spelce
1908–1998

Sometimes later in life people discover that they have a great talent that they did not know about, and that is just what happened to Fannie Spelce. Spelce was an outstanding nurse, but when she got older, she discovered that she was a very talented artist.

Spelce was born in Dyer, Arkansas, a little town at the foot of the Ozark Mountains. After completing four years of nursing training in Fort Smith, Arkansas, she spent a year in New York City sharpening her skills at the city's finest hospitals. She returned to Arkansas, married, and had two sons.

After a divorce, she worked in a number of small-town and big-city hospitals from Arkansas to California. To support her sons, Spelce often had two jobs. She worked the night shift at the hospital and came home long enough to give her sons breakfast. Then after taking her boys to school, she worked the day shift at the hospital.

In the 1950s, when doctors were performing pioneering heart operations at Methodist Hospital in Houston, Spelce was the nurse in charge of the operating room. She had a very important job, assisting doctors who were operating in a way that had never been done before. At the hospital Spelce was known as a dedicated nurse with a sharp eye for detail who could do anything.

In the late 1950s, she moved to Austin, Texas, and took a job as a nurse at a boarding school. She was on call twenty-four hours a day. The school gave her a year-round home in the school **infirmary** and vacation in the summer, when the students were gone.

Spelce had always wanted to draw, so one summer when a friend asked her if she would like to take an oil painting class at an art gallery, she quickly agreed. On the first day of class, the teacher arranged a **still life** and asked his students to paint it. Spelce spent the first part of the class working in a tiny area at the center of the canvas. When the teacher saw it, he told her that she was supposed to use the whole canvas. Spelce was so ashamed that she just could not start painting again. She spent the rest of the class cleaning her work from the canvas. She took the canvas home and painted the still life from memory. The next day she showed her picture to the teacher and shyly asked him if this was what she was supposed to do.

The teacher, Owen Cappleman, was amazed when he saw the painting. He told her that she was a natural artist with her own special style. He realized how talented she was and encouraged her to paint whatever she wanted. He advised Spelce not to take art lessons; she should develop her own painting style. Spelce loved painting her childhood memories, sometimes using old photographs as a guide. Her paintings had very carefully detailed **foregrounds** and **shimmering, impressionistic** backgrounds.

In 1966, Spelce painted *The Quilting Bee,* which showed a group of women making a quilt. It took her a year to complete. Using a magnifying glass and a single-hair brush, she painted the window curtains in the scene thread by thread. This became her best-known work.

When one of her sons took several of her paintings to New York City, to show to some art dealers, they were so impressed with her work that a bidding war broke out among them. It ended only when Spelce decided in which gallery she would like her paintings displayed. Her art dealer sold her work as folk art, which means that the art is made by people who wish to tell a story in art form even though they are untrained as artists.

For twenty years, she painted oil paintings filled with bright, strong details of life on an Arkansas farm. Like many natural artists, Spelce had an excellent memory and could remember childhood scenes exactly. Through her long nursing career, Spelce had never forgotten the farm she grew up on. In her paintings she brought to life loving memories. One painting shows a little girl playing hopscotch in a family yard. Spelce explained, "My mother wouldn't let me play hopscotch. Girls didn't kick up their heels then. It wasn't ladylike. So, I'd slip out when she didn't know it and do it anyway."

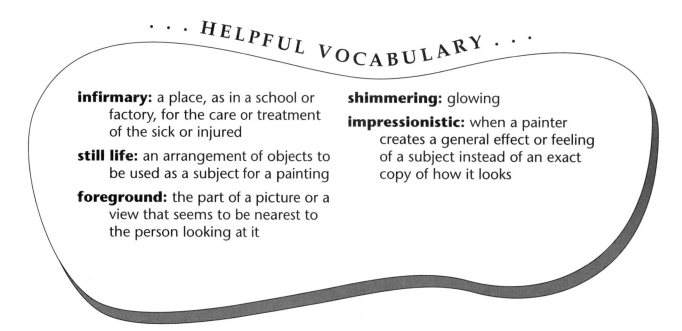

· · · HELPFUL VOCABULARY · · ·

infirmary: a place, as in a school or factory, for the care or treatment of the sick or injured

still life: an arrangement of objects to be used as a subject for a painting

foreground: the part of a picture or a view that seems to be nearest to the person looking at it

shimmering: glowing

impressionistic: when a painter creates a general effect or feeling of a subject instead of an exact copy of how it looks

THINKING ABOUT WHAT YOU HAVE READ

1. Where was Spelce born?

_____

_____

2. Why was Spelce's job at Methodist Hospital in Houston so important?

_____

_____

_____

3. How do you think Spelce's job at the private school was different from her work at Methodist Hospital?

_____

_____

_____

4. If Spelce was interested in drawing, why do you think it took her so long to sign up for an art class?

_____

_____

_____

5. What is folk art?

_____

_____

_____

6. Why do you think the teacher asked his students to draw a still life?

_____

_____

115

7. From the details given about Spelce's paintings in the story, do you think you would like them? Explain your answer.

_____

_____

_____

8. Besides paintings, what are other examples of folk art?

_____

_____

_____

WORKING WITH WORDS

An **antonym** is a word that has the opposite meaning of another word. *Famous* is the opposite of *unknown*. Write an antonym for each of the following words. Give yourself a bonus point if you can do the last two.

careful _____ _____

outstanding _____ _____

finest _____ _____

displayed _____ _____

ashamed _____ _____

complete _____ _____

private _____ _____

encourage _____ _____

Sometimes words have more than one meaning. In the following sentences, the word in bold print has one meaning. Write what it is. Then write another meaning the word may have. Give yourself a bonus point if you can do the last one.

Example: My grandfather likes to **rest** after dinner. In this sentence, *rest* means "to relax or take it easy." *Rest* can also mean "something that is left."

She **spent** a year in New York City.

_____

_____

_____

She **returned** to Arkansas.

_____

_____

_____

Did she **hang** the picture?

_____

_____

_____

She had lots of **free** time.

_____

_____

_____

After her divorce Fannie worked hard to **support** her sons.

_____

_____

_____

A **simile** is a phrase or expression introduced by the words _like_ or _as_; it compares two things that are not alike. For example, when Fannie held two jobs, she was _as busy as a bee_. See if you can use this simile in a sentence.

_____

_____

Now explain what these similes mean and use them in sentences. Give yourself a bonus point if you can do the last one.

Spelce had to be _as quick as a wink_ in the operating room.

_____

_____

_____

Her patients thought she was *as good as gold.*

_____

_____

_____

After a busy day at the hospital, Fannie was *as limp as a dishrag.*

_____

_____

_____

WRITING SKILLS

Spelce was very ashamed when she realized she had not done what the teacher wanted her to do. Describe a time when you saw someone do something that you think she or he should have been ashamed of.

First, write down some key ideas. When you have finished your paragraph, proofread your writing. Check it for correct spelling, grammar, capitalization, and punctuation.

Key ideas:

_____

_____

_____

Paragraph

_____

_____

_____

_____

_____

_____

_____

_____

Spelce had two careers. Fannie was an excellent nurse and later she became a fine artist. Write about two careers you think you might be interested in. Why are you interested in them?

Be sure that your paragraph has a topic sentence, which gives the main idea of the paragraph, and a concluding sentence, which lets the reader know that you have finished your discussion.

First, write down some key ideas. When you have finished your paragraph, proofread your writing. Check it for correct spelling, grammar, capitalization, and punctuation.

Key ideas:

_____

_____

_____

Paragraph

_____

_____

_____

_____

_____

_____

_____

_____

_____

In mid ocean, how do ship captains know where they are going?

_____

_____

Bettman/Corbis

John Harrison
1693–1776

A little over three hundred years ago, sailors did not know their location once they were out of sight of land. They needed two measurements to find exactly where they were—latitude and longitude. They could measure the latitude, how far north or south of the **equator** they had sailed. But there was no way for them to figure out their longitude, a sailor's distance east or west from an agreed place. Each year thousands of sailors lost their lives and many ship owners lost valuable **cargo** in shipwrecks caused by mistakes in navigation.

The British government knew that solving the longitude problem would save lives. So in 1714 it offered large prizes to anyone who could find a way to measure the distance east or west. The greatest reward would be 20,000 pounds (several million dollars in today's money). The government said that the longitude solution would have to be very exact, and it would be tested on a ship sailing over the ocean from Great Britain to any **port** in the West Indies. The government set up a Board of Longitude, which would judge and give out the rewards.

After more than thirty-five years of work John Harrison, an English clockmaker, finally solved the longitude problem and won the prize. He invented a very precise timepiece that could keep exact time at sea. What makes Harrison's story even more remarkable is that for the most part, he worked alone.

We do not know why Harrison became interested in making clocks. But we do know that in 1713, when he was twenty years old, he finished his first **pendulum** clock. During the 1720s Harrison built three clocks and solved some very important clockmaking problems. In those days the oils used in clocks were of poor quality. They were one of the major reasons that clocks did not work. But Harrison invented a clock that did not need oil. He also developed a way to keep his clocks from slowing down in warmer temperatures, something that happened often. His design changes made his clocks so accurate that they were never off by more than one second a month.

Harrison knew that if he could invent a clock that was as accurate on the sea as the clocks he made for land, this would solve the longitude puzzle. But he soon realized that no pendulum clock would work on the rolling sea. He knew, too, that the watches then used were even more incorrect.

To be accepted for the longitude prize, a timekeeper had to keep time with a change of no greater than 2.8 seconds a day. So Harrison decided that he would have to invent a clock that would not be affected by the motion of the ship nor by a change in temperature. For over twenty-eight years, he tried to invent such a clock. Harrison built three different models, each one better than the one before. He worked on the last one for nineteen years, but it still was not accurate enough.

Then in 1753, he realized what the solution was when he hired a London watchmaker to make him a watch for his own use. The watchmaker followed Harrison's own designs. Then Harrison finished and adjusted the watch. He discovered that one of the changes he had made in the design produced a timepiece that kept excellent time no matter how much it was moved about. This made him decide to build a watch rather than a portable clock to solve the longitude problem.

In 1755, Harrison asked the Board of Longitude for money "to make two watches one of such a size as may be worn in the pocket & the other bigger." The timekeeper that Harrison made looked very much like a very large pocket watch that we might see today. But the way he had designed it made it very resistant to shock and to changes in temperature and kept it running all the time.

Harrison asked the Board of Longitude if the watch could be tested. By this time Harrison's son William was working with his father. Finally, in 1761, a ship sailed to the West Indies with William Harrison and the watch on board. When the ship had to make an emergency stop, William, with the help of the watch, correctly predicted that the ship was nearly 100 miles closer to land than a ship's officer had thought. The captain was so impressed that he told Harrison he would like to buy the next watch he made.

As they sailed farther, William proved to the ship's company that their longitude was well over 100 miles different from what they figured it was. In addition, the watch was only 5.1 seconds slow.

But there was one problem. No one had discussed and agreed on the rate of the watch. The rate is the amount of time a watch could be fast or slow in a week or a month. Even very accurate timekeepers do not keep exact time. As long as the amount of time lost or gained is regular and predictable, it does not really matter. But for longitude trials, this idea was entirely new. Since the Harrisons had not declared the rate of the watch before leaving port, there was no way of knowing if it was as accurate as William said it was. So the trial did not count.

When William Harrison arrived back in England, he figured that the watch was in error by only 1 minute, 54.5 seconds for a period of 147 days. But the Board of Longitude were not convinced of William's figures. They agreed to give John Harrison 2,500 pounds. But one thousand of these pounds would be paid only after there was another trial. The Board found it hard to believe that a watch, which looked just like an ordinary watch, could be the solution to the complicated longitude question.

For the second trial, the watch was used again on a ship going to the West Indies. Again, the watch was a great success! Its performance was three times better than the performance needed to win the full 20,000 pounds of the prize. But when the Board met in 1765, they said they would give Harrison only enough money to make up the first half of the full reward. They wanted him to make at least two other watches that were similar to the first and to have them tested. They were afraid the first watch was just a lucky accident.

Although John Harrison was in his late seventies, he and his son continued working for the next two years on the first of the two timekeepers. But at the age of seventy-nine, Harrison decided that he was too old to make another watch. To receive the prize that he believed he had already earned, Harrison asked the most powerful person in the country for help, King George III. In a letter, he asked the king to put his watch on trial at his private **observatory.**

The king ordered Harrison to come to Windsor Castle to talk about his invention. At this meeting the king is said to have remarked: "These people have been cruelly wronged. . . . By God, Harrison, I will see you righted."

Even though Harrison's watch performed beautifully for the king, the Board of Longitude would not give Harrison the prize. They said the watch must pass an official trial. This was the last contact between the Board and Harrison. The prime minister then found a solution. By an act of parliament Harrison was awarded 8,750 pounds on June 21, 1773. Adding together all the money he had received earlier from the board, the final sum was a little bit more than the total 20,000 pounds.

At last Harrison had won, but more important to him than the money was that people knew he was the person who had solved the longitude problem. A few years later, on his eighty-third birthday, John Harrison died.

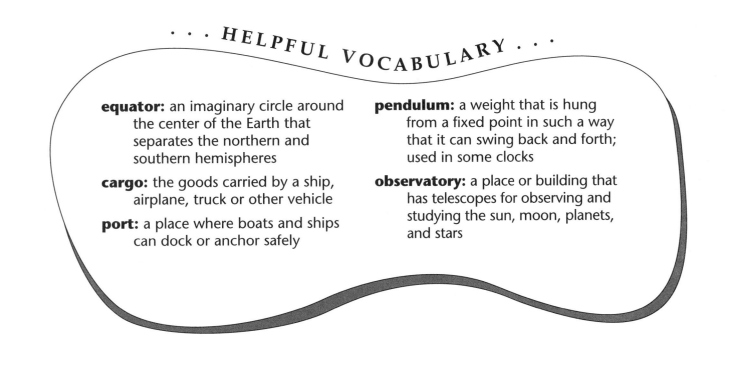

· · · HELPFUL VOCABULARY · · ·

equator: an imaginary circle around the center of the Earth that separates the northern and southern hemispheres

cargo: the goods carried by a ship, airplane, truck or other vehicle

port: a place where boats and ships can dock or anchor safely

pendulum: a weight that is hung from a fixed point in such a way that it can swing back and forth; used in some clocks

observatory: a place or building that has telescopes for observing and studying the sun, moon, planets, and stars

THINKING ABOUT WHAT YOU HAVE READ

1. Why was it so important for a sailor to be able to see land?

_____

_____

2. What is longitude?

_____

_____

_____

3. Why did the British government set up a longitude prize?

_____

_____

4. How long did it take John Harrison to win the longitude prize?

_____

_____

5. What was so amazing about Harrison's discovery?

_____

_____

_____

6. Why was Harrison's new pocket watch so important?

_____

_____

_____

7. Even though the watch was very accurate on the first trial, why was the trial useless?

_____

_____

_____

8. Why would the Board of Longitude not give Harrison the full reward after the second trial?

_____

_____

_____

9. How did King George III and the prime minister help Harrison?

_____

_____

_____

WORKING WITH WORDS

A **suffix** is a letter or group of letters that we place at the end of a word or word root to change its meaning. The suffix *-tion* means "state of" or "act of."

Example: *invention.* Could John Harrison *invent* a timepiece that could keep exact time at sea? Yes, it was a great *invention.*

List three words and then make new words by adding the suffix *-tion.*

direct   **direction**

_____   _____

_____   _____

_____   _____

The suffix *-ness* means "state or quality of being." List three words and then make new words by adding the suffix *-ness.*

rich   **richness**

_____   _____

_____   _____

_____   _____

A **proverb** is a short saying that expresses something that many people believe to be true. "Don't cry over spilled milk" is a proverb. It means do not worry about something that is past. Write answers to the questions below. If you can do the last one, give yourself a bonus point.

How was John Harrison's life an example of the proverb "Don't cry over spilled milk"?

_____

_____

_____

How do Harrison's experiments with his clock illustrate the proverb "Rome was not built in a day"?

_____

_____

_____

When King George III agreed to meet with John Harrison, he knew "there are two sides to every story." What does this proverb mean?

_____

_____

_____

Some words sound alike but are spelled differently and have different meanings. These words are called **homophones.**

Example: *right* and *write*. John Harrison knows he is *right* to ask for the prize. He will *write* to the king to ask for his help.

See if you can fill in the blanks with homophones. Be sure to read both sentences in the pair before you write your answers.

Do you think John Harrison had a big _____?

My dad is our Little League coach because he _____ so much about baseball.

Was it _____ the way the Longitude Board treated Harrison?

Do you think the bus _____ will be raised next year?

John Harrison often drank a cup of _____ in the morning.

The golfer always carries an extra _____ in his golf bag.

Many people could not believe that a clockmaker had _____ the Longitude Prize.

_____ day I hope I can go to Africa.

John Harrison turned _____ when he heard that the Longitude Board wanted another trial of his watch.

On a farm, milk was often carried in a _____.

Harrison had a lot of _____ and finally won the prize.

Many _____ are waiting for the doctor.

WRITING SKILLS

Before John Harrison's discovery, thousands of sailors died at sea. Write a notice telling people about the new Longitude Prize. Be sure you include all the important information needed to win the prize. Make an illustration to go with it, if you wish. But first, write down some key ideas. When you have finished, proofread your writing. Check it for correct spelling, grammar, capitalization, and punctuation.

Key ideas:

_____

_____

_____

Notice

_____

_____

_____

_____

_____

_____

_____

_____

_____

Illustration

Pretend that you are John Harrison. Write a letter to King George III asking to meet him. Be sure to include all the reasons why you think the meeting should take place. First, write down some key ideas. When you have finished, proofread your writing. Check it for correct spelling, grammar, capitalization, and punctuation.

Key ideas:

_____

_____

_____

Dear King George:

_____

_____

_____

_____

_____

_____

Sincerely,

John Harrison

You have just finished reading biographies of all kinds of people. Think about a person who is special to you. It can be a friend or someone in your family. It might even be a person you do not know. Think about what you know about this person's life. If you can, interview them. If it is someone you do not know, you might want to go to the library to do some reading. Then write a biography of this person. Be sure to write a title.

Key ideas:

_____

_____

_____

_____

_____

_____

_____

_____

_____

_____

_____

_____

_____

_____

_____

_____